OCCASIONAL PAPER 212

Financial Soundness Indicators:
Analytical Aspects and Country Practices

V. Sundararajan, Charles Enoch, Armida San José,
Paul Hilbers, Russell Krueger, Marina Moretti, and Graham Slack

D1364778

INTERNATIONAL MONETARY FUND
Washington DC
2002

Production: IMF Graphics Section
Figures: Joseph Kumar
Typesetting: Alicia Etchebarne-Bourdin

Cataloging-in-Publication Data

Financial soundness indicators: analytical aspects and country practices/
V. Sundararajan . . . [et al.]—Washington, D.C.: International Monetary Fund,
2002.

p. cm.—(Occasional paper, ISSN 0251-6365; NO. 212)
Includes bibliographical references.
ISBN 1-58906-086-5

1. Financial institutions—Auditing. 2. Bank examination. 3. International
Monetary Fund. I. Sundararajan, Vasudevan. II. International Monetary Fund.
III. Occasional paper (International Monetary Fund); no. 212.

HF5686.F46F35 2002

Price: US$20.00
(US$17.50 to full-time faculty members and
students at universities and colleges)

Please send orders to:
International Monetary Fund, Publication Services
700 19th Street, N.W., Washington, D.C. 20431, U.S.A.
Tel.: (202) 623-7430   Telefax: (202) 623-7201
E-mail: publications@imf.org
Internet: http://www.imf.org

recycled paper

Contents

Figures

Appendix Tables

The following symbols have been used throughout this paper:

. . . to indicate that data are not available;

— to indicate that the figure is zero or less than half the final digit shown, or that the item does not exist;

– between years or months (e.g., 2000–01 or January–June) to indicate the years or months covered, including the beginning and ending years or months;

/ between years (e.g., 2000/01) to indicate a fiscal (financial) year.

"Billion" means a thousand million.

Minor discrepancies between constituent figures and totals are due to rounding.

The term "country," as used in this paper, does not in all cases refer to a territorial entity that is a state as understood by international law and practice; the term also covers some territorial entities that are not states, but for which statistical data are maintained and provided internationally on a separate and independent basis.

Preface

The development of indicators of financial soundness responds to the need for better tools to assess financial systems' strengths and vulnerabilities. A broad search for tools and techniques to detect and prevent financial crises was prompted by the international financial turmoil of the late 1990s. More recent episodes of instability have further highlighted the importance of continuous monitoring of financial systems as a crisis prevention tool. The IMF has undertaken a number of initiatives in this area, notably in support of strengthened surveillance of member countries through the joint IMF-World Bank Financial Sector Assessment Program, launched in 1999. Initial efforts were aimed at identifying a broad set of prudential and macroeconomic variables that are relevant for assessing financial soundness—referred to as macroprudential indicators. More recent work has focused on a subset of these indicators—both aggregate bank balance sheet and income statement information, and aggregate indicators of financial fragility of nonfinancial firms and nonbank financial markets—referred to as financial soundness indicators (FSIs).

This paper brings forward recent advances in our understanding of financial soundness indicators with a view to supporting ongoing efforts by national authorities and private institutions worldwide to monitor financial system soundness. The paper also discusses the use of financial soundness indicators in the operational work of the IMF, and identifies significant gaps in knowledge and directions for further work. The material in this paper was originally prepared for discussions in the IMF Executive Board in June 2001.

The insights contained in this paper are the result of the efforts of many. In particular, we would like to express our appreciation for member countries' participation in the IMF *Survey on the Use, Compilation, and Dissemination of Macroprudential Indicators*, which helped to provide comprehensive information on country practices. A number of background documents by IMF staff and others referred to in this paper were also critical in distilling analytical lessons on the selection and use of the indicators. We would like to thank also Mahinder S. Gill, Alfredo M. Leone, Pamela Madrid, and Ewe-Ghee Lim for their inputs into this Occasional Paper; Jacqueline Irving and Lucy Ulrich of the External Relations Department for editing and production coordination; and Raja Hettiarachchi and Kiran Sastry for valuable research assistance. The views expressed in this paper are those of IMF staff and do not necessarily reflect the views of national authorities or of IMF Executive Directors.

<table>
<tr><td align="center">Carol S. Carson</td><td align="center">Stefan Ingves</td></tr>
<tr><td align="center">*Director*</td><td align="center">*Director*</td></tr>
<tr><td align="center">Statistics Department</td><td align="center">Monetary and Exchange Affairs
Department</td></tr>
</table>

List of Abbreviations

BIS	Bank for International Settlements
CAMELS	Capital adequacy, asset quality, management soundness, earnings, liquidity, sensitivity to market risk
CGFS	Committee on the Global Financial System, BIS
CPSS	Committee on Payment and Settlement Systems, BIS
EBIT	Earnings before interest and tax
EBITDA	Earnings before interest, tax, depreciation, and amortization
ECB	European Central Bank
FSAP	Financial Sector Assessment Program
FSI	Financial soundness indicator
FSSA	Financial System Stability Assessment
FX	Foreign exchange
G-7	Group of Seven
G-10	Group of Ten
GDP	Gross domestic product
IAIS	International Association of Insurance Supervisors
IMF	International Monetary Fund
IOSCO	International Organization of Securities Commissions
MPI	Macroprudential indicator
NBFI	Nonbank financial intermediary
NPL	Nonperforming loan
OECD	Organization for Economic Cooperation and Development
OTC	Over-the-counter
RAROC	Risk-adjusted return on capital
ROA	Return on assets
ROE	Return on equity
ROSC	Report on Observance of Standards and Codes
SDDS	Special Data Dissemination Standard
VaR	Value at Risk

I Overview

Structural, institutional, and macroeconomic aspects of financial system stability are receiving growing attention both nationally and in international fora. The magnitude and mobility of international capital flows have made it increasingly important to strengthen the foundations of domestic financial systems as a way to build up resilience to capital flow volatility. The soundness of financial institutions is also a key part of the infrastructure for strong macroeconomic performance and effective monetary policy at the national level. Hence, central banks and governments are paying increasing attention to monitoring the health and efficiency of financial institutions and markets, and to macroeconomic and institutional developments that pose potential risks to financial stability.

Such activities are typically embedded in central banks' mandates to promote financial stability and sound payment systems. They differ from financial supervisory activities insofar as they are primarily directed at a range of factors that may pose risks to the financial system as a whole—systemic risks—with significant macroeconomic repercussions. Financial supervisory tasks, on the other hand, are often focused more directly on the health of individual institutions. Given the linkages between microeconomic conditions and macroeconomic and overall financial stability, the monitoring of developments and policy responses to ensure financial stability poses special challenges, particularly when financial supervision functions are separated from the central bank.

The development of measures of financial sector soundness, and of methods to analyze them, are the subjects of this occasional paper. We refer to them as financial soundness indicators (FSIs) and macroprudential analysis, respectively (see Box 1.1). The IMF has been accumulating experience in these areas as part of its surveillance, technical assistance, and policy development work, and, more recently, in the context of the Financial Sector Assessment Program (FSAP).[1] An initial, relatively broad set of indica-

tors—the so-called macroprudential indicators—was identified in this earlier work, comprising aggregated prudential indicators, macroeconomic variables associated with financial system vulnerability, and market-based indicators. A consultative meeting on macroprudential indicators was held at IMF headquarters in September 1999. High-level experts from central banks, supervisory agencies, international institutions, academia, and the private sector discussed their experiences in using, measuring, and disseminating indicators of financial system soundness. An IMF Executive Board meeting in January 2000 discussed the state of knowledge in these areas and proposals for further work.[2] Recent Board papers on the Special Data Dissemination Standard (SDDS) and on the FSAP also discussed related issues.[3]

Discussions at the January 2000 review highlighted the need for more research and analysis to improve understanding of what determines financial system soundness and to deal with the considerable conceptual and statistical difficulties that arise in defining and compiling indicators of financial soundness. The Board recommended that the IMF conduct a survey of member countries on their needs and practices related to indicators of financial soundness. The Board also concurred on the need for better indicators on developments in specific sectors and markets that have proven to be relevant in assessing financial sector vulnerabilities, but that have been difficult to gauge in practice. These include nonbank financial institutions, the corporate sector, households, and real estate markets. Moreover, the Board pointed to the need to select a smaller and more operationally useful "core set" of indicators, intended to

---

[1]The FSAP was launched jointly by the IMF and the World Bank in May 1999. The program is designed to identify financial system strengths and vulnerabilities and to help to develop appropriate policy responses. Financial System Stability Assessments (FSSAs) are prepared by IMF staff in the context of Article IV consultations, by drawing on the FSAP findings, for discussion in the IMF Executive Board. In the World Bank, the FSAP reports provide the basis for producing Financial Sector Assessments and formulating financial sector development strategies. See IMF (2001a, b) and Hilbers (2001).

[2]See Evans, Leone, Gill, and Hilbers (2000).

[3]See IMF (2000c, 2001b).

Box 1.1. Definitions

Financial soundness indicators (FSIs) are indicators compiled to monitor the health and soundness of financial institutions and markets, and of their corporate and household counterparts. FSIs include both aggregated information on financial institutions and indicators that are representative of markets in which financial institutions operate. Macroprudential indicators include both FSIs and other indicators that support the assessment and monitoring of the strengths and vulnerabilities of financial systems, notably macroeconomic indicators.

Macroprudential analysis is the assessment and monitoring of the strengths and vulnerabilities of financial systems. This encompasses quantitative information from both FSIs and indicators that provide a broader picture of economic and financial circumstances, such as GDP growth and inflation, along with information on the structure of the financial system, qualitative information on the institutional and regulatory framework—particularly through assessments of compliance with international financial sector standards and codes, and the outcome of stress tests (see Figure 2.1 in Chapter II).

---

serve as a basis for structuring data work in support of financial system monitoring, including through the FSAP, and as a focal point for efforts by the IMF to encourage compilation and dissemination of macroprudential information by national authorities.

Since then, the IMF has substantially advanced the work on the measurement and analysis of financial soundness, including through activities in the context of the FSAP and the *Survey on the Use, Compilation, and Dissemination of Macroprudential Indicators*, conducted in the summer of 2000.[4] Efforts have been directed, in particular, to gauge the usefulness of specific indicators; identify analytically relevant definitions of these indicators; appraise compilation and dissemination practices among member countries; explore methods of macroprudential analysis, notably stress testing; and explore the role of nonbank financial intermediaries, the corporate sector, and real estate markets in assessing financial system vulnerabilities.

Other international organizations have also focused on these issues. For instance, the topic of the October 2000 Bank for International Settlements (BIS) annual meeting of central bank economists was *Marrying the Macro- and Micro-Prudential Dimensions of Financial Stability*.[5] At the European

Central Bank (ECB), the Working Group on Macroprudential Analysis of the Banking Supervision Committee received a mandate in 2000 to prepare semi-annual reports on macroprudential developments in Europe. These analyses, which are not made public, serve as input to discussions on financial stability issues in the ECB Governing Council. The Asian Development Bank has a program to collect and disseminate FSIs and related macroeconomic series for a group of Asian-Pacific countries. Similar efforts are ongoing at the national level in an increasing number of countries.[6]

This paper proposes two sets of indicators that are considered useful for the purpose of periodic monitoring, and for compilation and dissemination efforts by national authorities (Table 1.1). The *core set* includes indicators for the banking sector that should have priority in future compilation and monitoring of FSIs. The *encouraged set* includes additional banking indicators, as well as data on other institutions and markets that are relevant in assessing financial stability—the corporate sector, real estate markets, and nonbank financial institutions and markets. In particular, indicators of corporate health and of developments in real estate markets are considered a priority in light of their analytical significance for assessing financial vulnerabilities in a wide variety of circumstances. Their compilation, which is at present limited, should therefore be encouraged so that they could be included in the core set, in due course.

Working with two sets of FSIs—a core set and an encouraged set—avoids a one-size-fits-all approach, and provides a degree of flexibility in the selection of indicators that are most relevant to assessing vulnerabilities in country-specific circumstances. Indicators of the core set can be combined with selected, additional indicators of the encouraged set that might be of particular relevance in the country concerned, depending on its level of financial development, institutional structure, and regional circumstances.

Six criteria were applied in order to identify the core set, and some of those were applied to suggest the encouraged set: focus on core markets and institutions; analytical significance; revealed usefulness; relevance in most circumstances (i.e., not country-specific); availability; and parsimony—that is, achieving the maximum information content with a limited number of FSIs. The revealed usefulness and availability were judged based on the results of the survey noted earlier (see Part II), the analytical significance and parsimony were judged based on a survey of the literature as well as new empirical analysis

---

[4]The survey explicitly listed around 60 indicators, identified in earlier work.

[5]See www.bis.org/publ.

[6]In some countries—for instance, Finland, Hungary, Iceland, Norway, Sweden, and the United Kingdom—central banks publish special reports dealing with financial stability issues.

Table 1.1. Financial Soundness Indicators

	Core Set
Deposit-taking institutions	
Capital adequacy	Regulatory capital to risk-weighted assets
	Regulatory tier I capital to risk-weighted assets
Asset quality	Nonperforming loans to total gross loans
	Nonperforming loans net of provisions to capital
	Sectoral distribution of loans to total loans
	Large exposures to capital
Earnings and profitability	Return on assets
	Return on equity
	Interest margin to gross income
	Noninterest expenses to gross income
Liquidity	Liquid assets to total assets (liquid asset ratio)
	Liquid assets to short-term liabilities
Sensitivity to market risk	Duration of assets
	Duration of liabilities
	Net open position in foreign exchange to capital

	Encouraged Set
Deposit-taking institutions	Capital to assets
	Geographical distribution of loans to total loans
	Gross asset position in financial derivatives to capital
	Gross liability position in financial derivatives to capital
	Trading income to total income
	Personnel expenses to noninterest expenses
	Spread between reference lending and deposit rates
	Spread between highest and lowest interbank rate
	Customer deposits to total (noninterbank) loans
	Foreign currency-denominated loans to total loans
	Foreign currency-denominated liabilities to total liabilities
	Net open position in equities to capital
Market liquidity	Average bid-ask spread in the securities market[1]
	Average daily turnover ratio in the securities market[1]
Nonbank financial institutions	Assets to total financial system assets
	Assets to GDP
Corporate sector	Total debt to equity
	Return on equity
	Earnings to interest and principal expenses
	Corporate net foreign exchange exposure to equity
	Number of applications for protection from creditors
Households	Household debt to GDP
	Household debt service and principal payments to income
Real estate markets	Real estate prices
	Residential real estate loans to total loans
	Commercial real estate loans to total loans

[1]Or in other markets that are most relevant to bank liquidity, such as foreign exchange markets.

undertaken in the IMF on the definition, interpretation, and analysis of FSIs (see Part I). Both the survey and the analytical aspects were brought to bear in judging focus and country relevance.

Ideally, indicators included in the core and encouraged sets should also be comparable across countries—which would be possible if there existed in all areas internationally agreed prudential, accounting, and statistical standards to which all countries adhered—to facilitate monitoring of the financial system, not only at the national but also at the global level. The latter is important in view of the magnitude and mobility of international capital flows, and the risk of contagion of financial crises from one country to another. Advancing international comparability of FSIs and convergence toward best practice are important goals for further work in this area.

The review contained in this occasional paper highlights that work on measuring and analyzing FSIs has advanced substantially in recent years, and proposes specific areas where more work is needed.

- National authorities should be encouraged to compile and monitor FSIs systematically, based on available data.

- At the same time, guidelines are necessary to arrive at clear definitions of the indicators. Looking ahead, the IMF is working to produce, in consultation with national authorities and standard setters, a *Compilation Guide on Financial Soundness Indicators*.

- At the IMF, monitoring and analysis of FSIs should continue to be strengthened through the FSAP process and, more broadly, in the context of surveillance, technical assistance, and policy development work.

- Better indicators of the health of nonbank financial institutions and markets need to be developed—reflecting the specificities of each market segment—and of financial institutions' exposure to the household and real estate sectors.

- With regard to the corporate sector, data availability remains a key obstacle, particularly for non-listed companies, which represent a significant share of the sector in many countries. Further work to systematically compile FSIs of the nonfinancial corporate sector should be encouraged.

- Analytical tools that use FSIs need to be further developed, including more refined methods of aggregate stress testing of financial systems.

- Finally, the development of benchmarks for the level of FSIs would help monitor and interpret developments in the financial system, keeping in mind that benchmarks are most often country-specific and can change over time.

Monitoring and analysis of FSIs are just one element in an overall assessment of financial stability.

Other elements include analyses of macroeconomic developments, market-based data such as stock prices and credit ratings, structural information on the financial sector, and—last but not least—qualitative assessments, in particular assessments of observance of relevant international standards and codes. These elements, which feed into macroprudential analysis, will help to identify various dimensions of risks as well as the capacity of the system to cope with and manage these risks, thereby helping to form a judgment on overall financial stability. While these tools still remain imperfect and continue to evolve, over time, macroprudential analysis can reduce the incidence of crises by providing national authorities with a set of tools to comprehensively assess their financial sectors and identify weaknesses at an early stage.

The paper is organized in two parts—Part I focuses on selected analytical aspects of defining and analyzing FSIs, and Part II discusses country practices in the use, compilation, and dissemination of FSIs.

Within Part I, Chapter II introduces the framework of macroprudential analysis, including its quantitative as well as qualitative aspects, and reviews the experience with macroprudential analysis and indicators gained through the FSAP. Chapter III focuses on the definition and interpretation of indicators of the current health of the banking system, primarily derived by aggregating indicators of the health of individual banks. Indicators of specific sectors and markets that can have an impact on financial system stability—specifically, nonbank financial intermediaries (NBFIs), the corporate sector, households, and real estate markets—are discussed in Chapter IV. Chapter V looks at stress testing as a key component of macroprudential analysis.

Within the second part of this paper, Chapter VI introduces the *Survey on the Use, Compilation, and Dissemination of Macroprudential Indicators*. Chapter VII discusses survey results in terms of perceived usefulness of specific FSIs. Survey results on the compilation and dissemination of FSIs or their components are reported in Chapter VIII, and responses related to the analytical frameworks used by countries to analyze these indicators are reported in Chapter IX.

Chapter X concludes with proposals for a core set and an encouraged set of indicators to be used for the purpose of periodic monitoring, and for compilation and dissemination by national authorities. The chapter also discusses directions for further work on FSIs.

Part I

Selected Analytical Aspects

II   Indicators for Macroprudential Analysis

The Macroprudential Framework

Macroprudential analysis is a key building block of any policy framework for vulnerability analysis. It is a methodological tool that helps to quantify and qualify the soundness and vulnerabilities of financial systems.[7] It uses aggregated prudential data to obtain direct information on the current health of financial institutions; macroeconomic data to help set the analysis in the context of broader economic and financial trends; stress tests and scenario analysis to determine the sensitivity of the financial system to macroeconomic shocks; market-based information—such as prices and yields of financial instruments and credit ratings—as complementary variables conveying market perceptions of the health of financial institutions; and qualitative information on institutional and regulatory frameworks to help interpret developments in prudential variables. Structural data—including on the size of the main segments of the financial system, ownership structure, and concentration—typically supplement the analysis (Figure 2.1).

Of these broad categories of data—commonly referred to as macroprudential indicators—the focus of this paper is on aggregated prudential data and, to some extent, on selected market indicators. There is no universally accepted definition of macroprudential indicators. Broad definitions include all possible indicators related to financial system soundness, including relevant macroeconomic indicators (such as exchange and interest rates, and balance of payments data), and market-based indicators (such as stock prices of financial institutions, credit spreads, and credit ratings). This paper adopts, under the term "financial soundness indicators" (FSIs), a somewhat narrower definition, which includes mainly aggregated microprudential indicators of the health of financial institutions and indicators of the health of the major clients of financial institutions (the corporate and household sectors). This definition also in-cludes indicators of key developments in markets in which financial institutions operate—such as the breadth and depth of the money and capital markets, and developments in, and bank exposure to, the real estate markets.[8]

Macroprudential analysis closely complements and reinforces early warning systems and other analytical tools—currently in use or under development at the IMF—to monitor vulnerabilities and prevent crises. Early warning systems generally focus on vulnerabilities in the external position, using macroeconomic indicators as key explanatory variables.[9] Macroprudential analysis and the associated stress testing focus on vulnerabilities in domestic financial systems, using FSIs as the most significant statistical building block, and relate countries' financial sector soundness to macroeconomic, external, and capital account developments. Although FSIs and these analyses primarily aim to predict banking crises, they also provide an important input to more general vulnerability analyses and early warning systems. Their usefulness for these purposes will depend on the resolution of measurement and/or availability problems, which have so far made it difficult to incorporate them in vulnerability analysis systematically.[10]

An in-depth understanding of national financial systems requires intertemporal as well as cross-sectional analyses. Caution needs to be applied in both, however. Shifts in regulations such as accounting and provisioning norms can lead to breaks in time series and affect the robustness of intertemporal comparisons. Differing accounting, prudential, and

---

[7]Macroprudential analysis focuses on the health and stability of financial systems, whereas microprudential analysis deals with the condition of individual financial institutions.

[8]Macroeconomic indicators are not included in this definition, given their different source and character. They are, of course, part of the broader macroprudential analysis (see Figure 2.1), however, both as leading indicators of financial sector problems in their own right and as inputs into stress testing. See also Evans, Leone, Gill, and Hilbers (2000).

[9]See, in particular, Berg, Borensztein, Milesi-Ferretti, and Patillo (1999), and IMF (2000d).

[10]For the purpose of estimation of a robust early warning system, a variable must be reasonably comparable over time and across countries. See Berg, Borensztein, Milesi-Ferretti, and Patillo (1999).

Figure 2.1. Components of Macroprudential Analysis

FSIs

STRESS
TESTS

Macroeconomic
Data
eg., inflation, interest and
exchange rates

Macroprudential Analysis

Market-Based Data
eg., stock prices,
credit ratings

Qualitative
Information
eg., compliance
with standards

Structural
Information
eg., relative size,
ownership

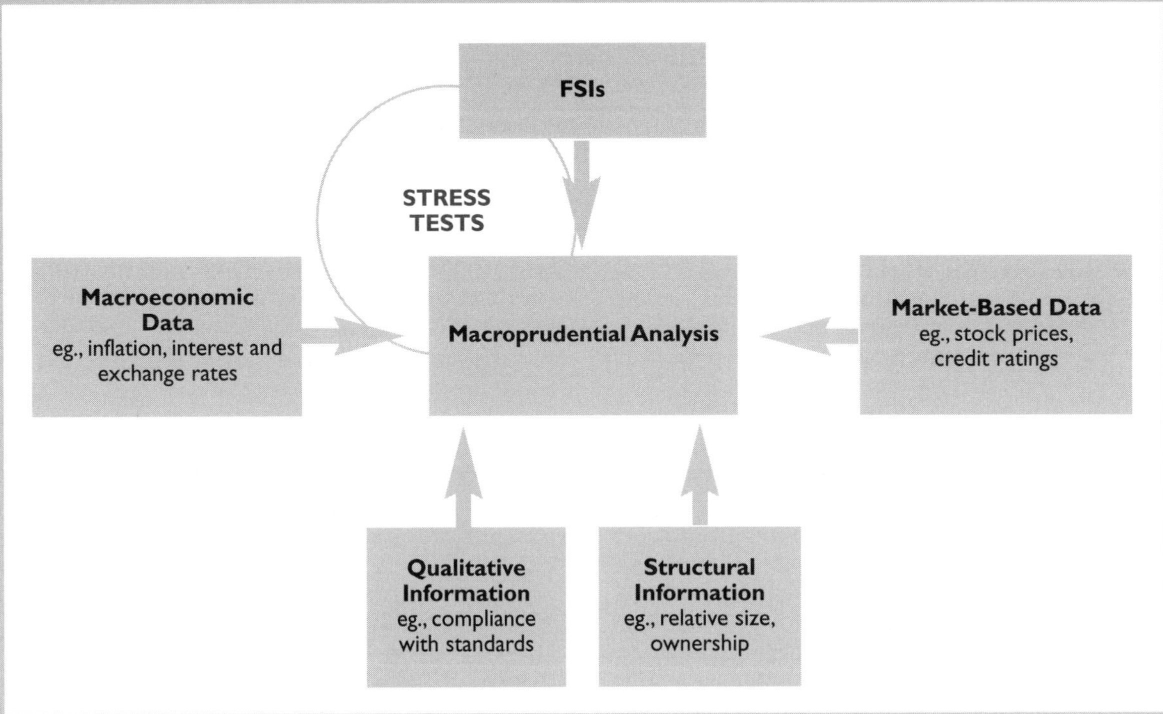

statistical standards, as well as differences in the structure of financial systems, typically make cross-country comparisons of FSIs difficult. Peer group analysis—the analysis of domestic intermediaries within a group (e.g., by size or market niche)—often provides important insights and can supplement cross-country comparisons. The use of benchmarks and thresholds for the level of FSIs would also help in analyzing FSIs. However, benchmarks are most often country-specific and shifts in their levels are difficult to discern as they occur.

FSIs in the Context of the FSAP

Macroprudential analysis is the basis for assessments of the soundness of financial systems that are carried out in the context of the FSAP and the related Financial System Stability Assessments (FSSAs). Financial sector assessments typically begin with an analysis of the macroeconomic environment and a description of the structure of the financial system. Within the financial system, the health of the banking sector is analyzed by looking at levels and trends in selected FSIs—typically of capital adequacy, asset quality, profitability, liquid-

ity, and exposure to market risks—and the linkage between these indicators and changes in the macroeconomic environment. In this sense, FSIs play a key role in FSSAs, which focus on financial stability issues and macro-financial linkages. Banking sector data, along with information on the rest of the financial system, bank borrowers (most commonly the corporate sector), and—when data availability allows—price trends in, and exposures to, real estate markets, typically serve as the basis for quantifying the vulnerability of the financial system. The combination of data analysis and other qualitative information (see above) is used to produce an overall assessment of the stability of the financial system.

The range of FSIs used in FSSAs has varied somewhat depending on the particular country case, but typically has followed some adaptation of the CAMELS framework.[11] An analysis of the indicators used in the FSSAs issued as of end-April 2001 (Table 2.1) shows that the most commonly used FSIs include, in order of frequency of use: (1) profitability indicators such as returns on assets and returns on

---

[11]Capital adequacy, asset quality, management soundness, earnings, liquidity, sensitivity to market risk.

equity, interest margin ratios, and noninterest income and expenses ratios; (2) asset quality indicators, notably nonperforming loan (NPL) ratios and provisions; (3) capital adequacy ratios, in particular the ratio of regulatory (Basel) capital to risk-weighted assets; (4) sensitivity to market risk indicators, notably open foreign exchange exposures; and (5) liquidity ratios. A limited number of FSSAs also looked at indicators of vulnerability in the corporate sector and one of the FSSAs included a more detailed analysis of the financial position of households (net worth, net financial assets, and stocks to total assets). Two reports included data on real estate (nonperforming mortgage loans, real estate collateral values, and real estate prices).

The selection and use of FSIs reflect several limitations. First, data for compiling indicators appeared to be often unavailable or available with only short consistently collected histories. As a result, the time series used in most FSSAs were limited in length. Second, compilation practices for FSIs varied significantly across countries, due to differing prudential, accounting, and statistical standards, thereby limiting the possibility of cross-country comparisons. Nonetheless, some reports present cross-country comparisons—with the usual caveat that not all indicators are strictly comparable—in an attempt to benchmark FSIs to those in other countries at similar levels of financial development. Despite the limitations, FSIs were generally considered useful as a way of organizing the analysis and potentially fostering better data collection and quality in the future.[12] With varying complexity, all FSSAs included stress testing of financial institutions' resilience to macroeconomic shocks. Commonly used shocks included a slowdown in economic growth, balance of payments shocks, and changes in inflation, interest, and exchange rates. In some of the more sophisticated models, asset price developments and contagion effects were used as channels through which shocks transmitted to financial institutions.

Qualitative Aspects

In carrying out financial sector assessments, it is important to evaluate how risk is managed by risk-taking units and how risk management is governed by regulatory authorities.[13] Different financial institutions have different risk appetites. Moreover, the level of risk-taking is strongly influenced by the particular institutional and regulatory framework of the financial system.

As absolute risk levels may not by themselves fully indicate financial institutions' or a system's vulnerabilities, an implicit concept of "net risk" is often applied to the assessment of financial institutions' or system vulnerabilities.[14] This concept allows combining the quantitative and qualitative aspects of financial vulnerability.[15] The "net risk" approach involves quantitatively evaluating all risks faced by financial institutions (including the direction of the risk assumed) and qualitatively adjusting for institutional characteristics to assess the extent to which the risks are adequately managed through market discipline and internal governance in an institution, and through regulatory and supervisory frameworks in the system as a whole. Such analyses can be synthesized into an overall risk assessment for individual institutions, and an overall stability assessment for the financial system, which evaluate the quantity of all risks against the quality of the institutions and institutional arrangements.[16] By definition, however, combining qualitative and quantitative aspects of risk is not an exact method and requires judgment.

Incentives

There are many institutional characteristics of a financial system that must be considered for qualitative adjustments to gross risk. The nature of government subsidies and taxes, payment culture and insolvency regime, credit and deposit guarantees, the quality of supervision and regulation, moral hazard, corporate governance, and management quality all affect the overall incentive structure of a financial system and must be taken into account in qualitative adjustments.[17]

---

[12]See Carson (2001) for a discussion of the factors affecting data quality.

[13]The linkages between the development of a sound banking system and well-functioning banking regulation and supervision are discussed in Sundararajan (1999). See also Sundararajan, Marston, and Basu (2001).

[14]For a description of a "net risk" approach to risk assessment in the context of dynamic banking supervisory practices, see Office of the Superintendent of Financial Institutions (1999).

[15]The importance of a healthy balance of quantitative and qualitative information in order to provide a meaningful picture of the extent and nature of financial risks has been recently highlighted by the Multidisciplinary Working Group on Enhanced Disclosure of the Financial Stability Forum (2001).

[16]It should be noted, however, that regulatory factors could influence the size and movement of FSIs, notably through the establishment of minimum regulatory ratios.

[17]The incentive audit approach, outlined by Chai and Johnston (2000), looks at three factors that affect the risk-taking and monitoring behavior of participants (investors, borrowers, and intermediaries) at the core of the financial system: (1) market structure and the availability of financial instruments that affect market discipline; (2) government safety nets, including implicit and explicit exchange rate and deposit/investor guarantees; and (3) the legal and regulatory framework, including high quality enforcement.

Table 2.1. FSIs Used in Financial System Stability Assessments

	Cameroon	Canada	Colombia	El Salvador	Estonia	Hungary	Iceland	India	Iran	Ireland	Kazakhstan	Lebanon	Peru	Poland	South Africa	Yemen
Capital adequacy																
Regulatory capital to risk-weighted assets[1]		X	X	X	X	X	X	X		X		X	X	X	X	X
Tier I capital to risk-weighted assets[2]		X				X	X	X		X	X	X	X		X	
Capital to assets	X		X	X		X	X	X		X	X	X				X
Asset quality																
(a) Lending institutions																
Loans (or credit) by sector		X	X	X	X	X	X			X				X		X
Large exposures to assets (or capital)						X	X		X							X
NPLs to gross loans (or to total assets)[3]	X	X	X	X	X	X	X	X		X	X	X	X	X	X	X
FX NPLs to gross FX loans				X	X								X			
Provisions (plus collateral values) to NPLs		X	X	X	X	X	X	X		X		X		X	X	X
Provisions to gross loans	X	X	X	X	X	X				X	X	X	X	X	X	
NPLs net of provisions ratios[4]								X								
Loans to collateral values			X													X
(b) Borrowing institutions																
Total debt to equity		X	X	X												
Return on average equity (ROE)		X	X	X												
Earnings to debt service			X													
External debt to total debt						X								X		
Earnings																
Return on average assets (ROA)[5]	X	X	X	X	X	X	X	X	X	X	X	X	X	X	X	X
Return on average equity (ROE)	X	X	X	X	X	X	X	X		X	X	X	X	X	X	X
Interest margin ratios[6]		X	X	X		X		X		X	X	X	X		X	
Noninterest income ratios[7]		X	X			X		X		X	X	X			X	
Noninterest expenses ratios[8]		X	X	X		X	X	X	X	X	X	X	X	X	X	
Personnel cost ratios[9]			X			X						X	X	X	X	
Liquidity																
Liquid asset ratios[10]		X	X	X	X	X				X	X	X	X	X	X	X
Loans (or deposits) to total assets			X													
Loans to deposits	X	X		X		X	X				X	X	X	X	X	X
Loans and/or deposits by currency	X	X	X			X	X			X	X	X	X	X	X	X
Central bank credit to total bank liabilities						X			X		X			X		

Volatility ratio[11]

Interbank turnover ratio and
bid/ask spread

Sensitivity to market risks

Duration of assets and liabilities

Net open FX position

---

[1] In one case, capital net of provisioning gap (NPLs minus provisions) was calculated as a share of risk-weighted assets.

[2] In one report, tiers 1 and 2 were expressed in domestic currency levels rather than as a ratio.

[3] In two cases, foreclosed assets or restructured loans were added to the NPL figure.

[4] Ratios to loans, or tier 1 capital, or gross income.

[5] One report looked at the risk-adjusted return on capital (RAROC), defined as ratio of interest margin to assets multiplied by the potential loss.

[6] Ratios to total interest income, or total average assets, or average net assets, or interest earning assets.

[7] Ratios to total income, or average net assets, or interest income.

[8] Ratios to total noninterest expenses, or average net assets.

[9] Noninterest income per employee; profits per employee; loans per employee; and deposits per employee. One report looked at profits per branch.

[10] Ratios of liquid assets to total assets, to deposits, to short-term liabilities, to total liabilities.

[11] Calculated as total volatile liabilities (total borrowed funds) net of liquid assets to total assets net of liquid assets.

An important aspect of the incentive structure is the legal framework. As all financial instruments are legal contracts, enforceability, recourse, and net expected returns are highly dependent upon a financial system's legal framework. If a country has a well-established commercial law with a court system well versed in financial litigation, legal risk is minimal. If it is not, qualitative adjustments to gross risk for these factors are essential.

Even well-functioning legal systems require qualitative adjustments of risk. There are underlying differences of financial contract enforceability among common and codified legal systems. Such differences also affect the accounting systems used, and from which financial soundness indicators are derived. Differences in accounting information for common versus codified legal systems are derived in part from differences in stakeholders in economies with the two legal foundations. Under a common law system, the principal stakeholder is the corporate shareholder. Under a codified legal system, creditors, labor, government, and other interested parties may be the relevant stakeholders. Different stakeholders require different information, which affects construction of financial ratios.[18]

Assessing the incentive structure should also take into account the objectives of managers, owners, and directors of financial institutions. Such objectives may differ and profit maximization may not always be the main objective. An example of where differences can affect financial institutions' vulnerability is in the area of lending. Bank managers interested in expanding business may reward employees by a percentage of loan volume contracted. Since loan quality is typically determined much later in the process, such behavior can lead to strong loan growth and income in the short run, with deterioration in loan quality and shareholder capital later on.

Observance of Standards and Codes

Assessments of observance and implementation of relevant financial sector codes, good practices, and standards help to capture key qualitative aspects of financial system stability, and are needed to supplement quantitative assessments carried out in macroprudential analysis. Such assessments, in particular, capture how financial system risk is managed through regulatory and supervisory frameworks by analyzing the extent to which observance of existing standards helps to address the identified vulnerabilities and risks. Such analyses are routinely carried out as part of the FSAP/FSSA process.[19] In this context, they have helped countries to focus on key operational and supervisory risks and to identify needed corrective actions and institutional strengthening plans. They can also help to reveal the quality of FSIs—for instance, of capital adequacy ratios through the assessment of compliance with the Basel Core Principles for Effective Banking Supervision.

The standards that have been assessed to date in the context of the FSAP/FSSA process—with country-specific prioritization of which standards were most relevant for assessment in each case—have been the Code of Good Practices on Transparency in Monetary and Financial Policies, the Basel Core Principles for Effective Banking Supervision, the Core Principles for Systemically Important Payment Systems, the International Organization of Securities Commissions (IOSCO) Objectives and Principles of Securities Regulation, and the International Association of Insurance Supervisors (IAIS) Insurance Core Principles. In selected cases, the Organization for Economic Cooperation and Development (OECD) Principles of Corporate Governance have also been assessed in the context of the FSAP.

Monitoring information on implementation of standards can be a useful component of financial system vulnerability analysis. A high degree of observance of relevant standards contributes to the stability of financial systems that are integrated into global financial markets and face a variety of financial innovations and shocks. Standards assessments are also helpful in identifying and implementing regulatory and operational reforms needed for the development of countries' financial systems over time and their integration into global markets.

---

[18]See, for example, Ball (2001).

[19]While FSAP reports provide detailed assessments of strengths and vulnerabilities, observance of standards, institutional structures, and overall stability and developmental needs, the focus of FSSAs is on financial system stability issues of significance for macroeconomic performance and policies. For details, see IMF (2001b). Summary assessments of financial sector standards and codes from the FSAP process are included in the FSSA and are also issued as Reports on Observance of Standards and Codes (ROSCs). See IMF (2001c).

III   Banking System

Bank Behavior and Vulnerabilities

Financial systems are exposed to a variety of risks, and the extent of exposure to these risks depends on the portfolio characteristics of individual banks, their systemic importance, the linkages with other institutions and markets, as well as the size and nature of the risks. Typically, an individual portfolio will be vulnerable to shocks to credit risk, liquidity risk, and market risk (including interest rate, exchange rate, equity price, and commodity price risks). Market risk and credit risk shocks can affect the portfolios of financial institutions either directly through changes in the value of financial assets that are marked-to-market, or indirectly through changes in the financial position of debtors that reduce credit quality. Shocks to depositor or investor confidence may create liquidity problems that also affect the balance sheets of financial institutions. These shocks are eventually reflected in the profitability and capital adequacy of financial institutions. Financial system vulnerability increases when shocks hit portfolios that are not liquid, hedged, or sufficiently diversified, and when there is insufficient capital to absorb the shocks.[20]

Recent papers have attempted to deepen our knowledge of financial institutions' characteristics and behavior that may increase the probability of crises. In their study based on work done for the South Africa FSAP mission, Barnhill, Papapanagiotou, and Schumacher (2000) conclude that while market risk, credit risk, portfolio concentration, and asset/liability mismatches are all important risk factors, in many countries credit quality is the most important source of vulnerability during periods of financial stress. Hence, particularly in the less sophisticated financial systems, the main channel through which shocks affect the risk profile of financial institutions is a collapse in borrowers' creditworthiness. These results point to the need to emphasize,

in the selection of a core set of FSIs, the quality of the loan portfolio of financial institutions, while at the same time monitoring the importance of nonlending activities in the generation of bank income.

Cortavarría, Dziobek, Kanaya, and Song (2000) review evidence that bank behavior may actually amplify financial crises.[21] Procyclical effects can be transmitted through three channels: capital, credit, and provisions. In times of recession, banks are likely to incur higher levels of loan losses, and consequently lower capital, than when the economy is strong. Moreover, retained earnings from bank profits, which add to Tier 1 capital, also tend to fall during a recession and rise in boom periods. Evidence of procyclical behavior through shifts in credit supply can be found in the credit crunch literature, which postulates that increased risk perceptions during a crisis and a shortage of bank capital lead to downward shifts in the supply of loans.[22] On the other hand, loan standards typically become more relaxed during economic expansions. A complicating factor in almost all the empirical evidence on this issue is the regulatory response during banking distress (tightening regulations), which may itself produce a procyclical effect during a downturn. From a policy perspective, however, this regulatory response is often intended to bring credit expansion to a more sustainable path.

Provisioning systems with a focus on ex post factors (such as interest past due) may also amplify financial crises. During an expansion, default rates typically fall, and banks relying mainly on ex post criteria respond by reducing the level of provisions, showing higher profits, and distributing more dividends. During the contraction that follows, when default rates rise, banks are suddenly faced with the need for higher provisions, which reduce capital, financial strength, and the ability to lend, thus contributing to a protracted downturn. Although empirical evidence of these effects is rather weak, provi-

---

[20]Systemic liquidity provision and the functioning of interbank markets can also affect the ability of the system to absorb shocks.

[21]For a recent discussion of procyclicality in the financial system, see also Borio, Furfine, and Lowe (2001).

[22]See for instance Agénor, Aizenman, and Hoffmaister (2000).

sioning may indeed provide incentives for banks to engage in procyclical behavior.

Delgado, Kanda, Mitchell Casselle, and Morales (2000) highlight that the availability of foreign currency loans to domestic borrowers influences the assessment of risks. Banks generally transfer currency risk to borrowers who commit to debt-service payments in foreign currency, regardless of the currency denomination of their revenue. This exposure compounds credit and currency risks, however: by not refinancing or hedging the obligation, the borrower remains exposed to an exchange rate risk that translates into a credit risk to the lender. Counterparty exposure also results from the risk that the domestic currency market value of the collateral backing the obligation declines. In this case, the borrower does not face direct exchange rate risk; however, the bank is exposed to a potential credit risk in the event of industry- or company-specific adversities, as the collateral no longer covers the obligation. Because the same demand factors often support domestic activities and asset prices (see Chapter IV), it is not unusual that countries experience both effects simultaneously.

Dziobek, Hobbs, and Marston (2000) analyze the determinants of bank liquidity—defined as the degree to which a financial institution is able to meet its obligations under normal business conditions. Volatility in the depositor (and creditor) base depends on the type of depositor, insurance coverage, and maturity. Banks that rely on a narrow or highly volatile funding base are more prone to liquidity squeezes. Household deposits are typically more stable than, for instance, the deposits of institutional investors or corporate entities. Deposit concentration (i.e., fewer, larger-sized deposits) can also be indicative of volatility. Deposit insurance increases the stability of the deposits it covers, with the important caveat that insurance schemes that are not credible may not have this effect. On the external front, foreign financing (for instance, through commercial credit lines), and deposits of nonresidents (either in foreign or domestic currency) can become highly volatile in situations of distress and make the financial system vulnerable to external shocks or adverse developments in the domestic economy. As regards instrument maturity, the longer the time before the liability matures (in terms of remaining maturity), the more stable the funding is. However, in countries where banks are required to meet early withdrawal requests with only minor penalties, maturity may be less relevant in determining funding stability.

Ultimately, the liquidity properties of assets and liabilities depend on a country's liquidity infrastructure and the resulting systemic liquidity. Dziobek, Hobbs, and Marston (2000) develop a framework for assessing the adequacy of arrangements for market liquid-

ity. The components of a balanced liquidity infrastructure are largely institutional in nature—including the existence of legal contract rights and information disclosure. Prevailing monetary arrangements, design aspects of central bank instruments, and arrangements for payments and money market operations also bear directly on banks' ability to manage short-term liquidity. For instance, high transaction costs resulting from rigid instrument design and trading rules can discourage trades and contribute to price volatility. Foreign exchange regulations—such as capital controls and prudential controls on open foreign currency positions—can affect access to foreign currency liquidity. For example, overly tight limits on net positions in foreign exchange can constrain banks' ability to manage liquidity through currency conversion. Restrictions on the use of currency derivatives may limit the incentive for developing hedging mechanisms that can improve management of liquidity and other types of risks.

Bank involvement in off-balance-sheet activities also has implications for systemic financial risks. Schinasi, Craig, Drees, and Kramer (2000) review the key features of modern banking and, in particular, over-the-counter (OTC) derivatives markets that are relevant for assessing their soundness.[23] Internationally active financial institutions have become exposed to additional sources of instability because of their large and dynamic exposures to credit risks embodied in their OTC derivatives activities. Although modern financial institutions still derive most of their earnings from intermediating, pricing, and managing credit risk, they are doing increasingly more of it off-balance-sheet. For example, a simple swap transaction is a two-way credit instrument in which each counterparty is both a creditor and a debtor. But there are important differences compared with traditional banking. The credit exposures associated with derivatives are time varying and depend on the price of underlying assets. Hence, financial institutions need to assess the potential change in the value of the credit extended (by marking it to market), and form expectations about the future path of the underlying asset price. This, in turn, requires an understanding of the underlying asset markets. Moreover, Breuer (2000) notes that off-balance-sheet positions can build up financial institutions'

---

[23]Compared with exchange-traded derivatives markets, OTC derivatives markets—in which transactions are not cleared through a centralized clearinghouse—have the following features: management of credit risk is decentralized at the level of individual institutions; there are no formal centralized limits on individual positions, leverage, or margining; there are no formal rules for risk and burden sharing; and there are no formal rules or mechanisms for ensuring market stability and integrity. On OTC derivatives markets, see also IMF (2000b), Chapter IV.

leverage that is not explicitly recorded on-balance-sheet. The creditor and debtor relationships implicit in OTC derivatives transactions between financial institutions can create situations in which the possibility of isolated defaults can threaten access to liquidity of key market participants—similar to a traditional bank run. The rapid unwinding of positions, as all counterparties run for liquidity, is characterized by creditors demanding payment, selling collateral, and putting on hedges, while debtors draw down capital and liquidate other assets. This can result in extreme market volatility.

Banking Indicators

The variety of risks to which banks are exposed justifies looking at aspects of bank operations that can be categorized under the CAMELS framework. This involves the analysis of six groups of indicators of bank soundness: capital adequacy, asset quality, management soundness, earnings, liquidity, and sensitivity to market risk. This section looks at specific indicators within these categories, with two caveats. First, management soundness is not dealt with explicitly in the section. Although this aspect is key to bank performance and, to some extent, is reflected in financial institutions' accounts, its evaluation is primarily a qualitative exercise, and its analysis is an integral part of banking supervision. Second, measurement of bank off-balance-sheet positions will be dealt with both under capital adequacy (as they affect leverage) and under asset quality (as they affect credit risk).

Although implicitly the indicators reviewed in this section refer to the consolidation of bank accounts at the national level, it is important to note that, for internationally active banks, the assessment of soundness should ideally include the consolidation of financial statements of foreign branches and affiliates. In this regard, as Baldwin and Kourelis (forthcoming) point out, analysts should be aware of potential differences across national boundaries in the treatment of loan-loss provisioning, asset and liability valuation, recognition of income and expenses, and deferral of gains and losses. Due attention should be paid to the accounting standards used in each country, and consolidation should be performed following uniform accounting standards.

Capital Adequacy

Capital adequacy and availability ultimately determine the robustness of financial institutions to shocks to their balance sheets. Aggregate risk-based capital ratios (the ratio of regulatory capital to risk-weighted assets) are the most common indicators of

capital adequacy, based on the methodology agreed to by the Basel Committee on Banking Supervision in 1988.[24] Simple ratios of capital to assets without differential risk weights often complement this measure. An adverse trend in these ratios may signal increased risk exposure and possible capital adequacy problems. In addition to the amount of capital, it may also be useful to monitor indicators of capital quality. In many countries, bank capital consists of different elements that have varying availability and capability to absorb losses, even within the broad categories of tier 1, tier 2, and tier 3 capital.[25] If these capital elements can be reported separately, they can serve as more reliable indicators of the ability of banks to withstand losses, and help to put overall capital ratios into context.

The Basel Committee's minimum standards for risk-weighted capital adequacy were originally intended to apply only to internationally active banks, but are now used in most countries—industrial, emerging, and developing—and for most banks (see Box 3.1). Recent proposals have been put forward by the Basel Committee to update this standard, to account for the rapid development of new risk-management techniques and financial innovation.[26] These proposals introduce greater refinement into the existing system of risk weighting, to relate its categories more accurately to the economic risks faced by banks—including as measured by banks' own internal ratings systems, or, less elaborately, based on ratings from external rating agencies. However, improved risk measurement comes at the expense of comparability. Under the new proposal, each bank's way of estimating credit risk can differ, which, being reflected in different risk-weighted assets and capital ratios, would make aggregation of individual bank ratios problematic. This issue has not so far been tackled explicitly in the Basel proposal.

Well-designed loan classification and provisioning rules are key to obtaining a meaningful capital ratio. Loan classification rules determine the level of provisioning, which affects capital both indi-

---

[24]The Basel Committee's 1988 risk measurement framework assigns all bank assets to one of four risk-weighting categories, ranging from zero to 100 percent, depending on the credit risk of the borrower. The Basel Capital Accord requires internationally active banks in Bank for International Settlements (BIS) member countries to maintain a minimum ratio of capital to risk-adjusted assets of 8 percent.

[25]Tier 1 capital consists of permanent shareholders' equity and disclosed reserves; tier 2 capital consists of undisclosed reserves, revaluation reserves, general provisions and loan-loss reserves, hybrid debt-equity capital instruments, and subordinated long-term debt (over five years); tier 3 capital consists of subordinated debt of shorter maturity (two to five years). See Basel Committee (1988, 1998).

[26]See Basel Committee (2001).

Box 3.1. Basel Capital Adequacy Ratio

The Basel capital adequacy ratio was adopted in 1988 by the Basel Committee on Banking Supervision as a benchmark to evaluate whether banks operating in the G-10 countries have sufficient capital to survive likely economic shocks. The ratio calls for minimum levels of capital to (i) provide a cushion against losses due to default arising from both on- and off-balance-sheet exposures; (ii) demonstrate that bank owners are willing to put their own funds at risk; (iii) provide quickly available resources free of transactions and liquidation costs; (iv) provide for normal expansion and business finance; (v) level the playing field by requiring universal application of the standard to internationally active banks; and (vi) encourage less risky lending.

The original Basel capital ratio, along with subsequent amendments, requires international banks to have a specific measure of capital greater than or equal to 8 percent of a specific measure of assets weighted by their estimated risk. The ratio is an analytical construct with complex definitions of the numerator (capital) and the denominator (risk-weighted assets) that cannot be derived directly from standard financial statements. The formula states that a banking enterprise must have capital on a worldwide consolidated basis equal to 8 percent or more of its risk-weighted assets, which includes off-balance-sheet positions.

$$\frac{\text{Risk-based Capital}}{\text{Adequacy Ratio}} = \frac{\text{Capital} \times 100}{\text{Risk-Weighted Assets}} \leq 8$$

where: Capital = (tier 1 Capital – Goodwill) + (tier 2 Capital) + (tier 3 Capital) – Adjustments

Tier 1 capital, or "core capital," consists of equity capital and disclosed reserves that are considered freely available to meet claims against the bank.

Tier 2 capital consists of financial instruments and reserves that are available to absorb losses, but which might lack permanency, have uncertain values, might entail costs if sold, or otherwise lack the full loss-absorption capacity of tier 1 capital items.

Tier 3 capital consists of subordinated debt with an original maturity of at least two years for use, if needed, against market risk exposures associated with fluctuations in the market value of assets held.

Goodwill is subtracted because the value of goodwill may fall during crises, and various adjustments are made to capital to prevent possible double counting of value.

Risk-weighted assets, the denominator, are the weighted total of each class of assets and off-balance-sheet asset exposures, with weights related to the risk associated with each type of asset. In the example given in the table below, the book value of assets is 940, but the value of risk-weighted assets is 615.

Example of Estimation of Risk-Weighted Assets

Type of Asset	Value of Holdings	Risk weight	Result
U.S. Treasury bonds	200	0 %	0
Mortgage loans	250	50 %	125
Corporation bonds	120	100 %	120
Consumer loans	370	100 %	370
Total	940	—	615

Capital adequacy ratios are often not directly comparable between countries because national supervisors have some leeway in defining weights and adjustments and, even more importantly, national practice may vary in the valuation of assets, recognition of loan losses, and provisioning, which can significantly affect the ratio. Moreover, an aggregate measure of capital adequacy potentially disguises information on individual institutions; thus, for macroprudential analysis, it is useful to supplement the aggregate ratio with information on the dispersion of ratios for individual institutions or subsectors of the banking system.

Recent developments in the ratio include attempts to refine the weighting system. In particular, the Basel Committee has a proposal to revamp the standard to permit greater differentiation between assets based on their risk, including the possibility of using (under limited conditions) internal model-based measures of risk exposures.

rectly (by reducing income) and directly (through inclusion of general provisions, to some extent, in regulatory capital).[27] Moreover, in most Group of Ten (G-10) countries, banks are required to deduct specific provisions (or loan-loss reserves) from loans—that is, credit is calculated on a *net* basis— which reduces the value of total assets and hence of capital (see Box 3.2).[28]

Simple gearing ratios—the ratio of capital to assets, without differential risk weights—are also meaningful indicators and are often used, as

---

[27]The Basel Capital Accord allows banks to include general provisions in tier 2 capital, up to 1.25 percent of (risk) assets.

[28]Although accounting and prudential standards usually require the deduction of provisions from loans, international statistical standards recommend recording loans gross of provisions until the loan is written off.

┌───┐

Box 3.2. Valuation of Capital

Bank capital (or equity) equals assets minus lia-bilities. Since capital is a residual, it cannot be mea-sured directly and its quantification requires that each item affecting its level be evaluated—includ-ing assets, liabilities, off-balance-sheet commit-ments, and other items. The valuation of assets is the most important component and different meth-ods are needed to evaluate the main categories of assets (loan portfolio, securities, fixed assets, other assets). Methodological issues include: (1) market value versus book value, (2) replacement value ver-sus yield-based value, and (3) going concern value versus liquidation value. Valuation of liabilities is more straightforward, although the valuation of some elements of tier 2 regulatory capital (notably subordinated debt and hybrid instruments) may be complicated. The impact of off-balance-sheet items on capital is particularly difficult to evaluate be-cause of the mostly contingent nature of these items. Finally, a wide range of other items must be taken into account, including hidden reserves and losses in the form of unbooked transactions, good-will, franchise value, and financial damages and penalties linked with pending legal cases.

└───┘

Cortavarría, Dziobek, Kanaya, and Song (2000) point out.

The analysis in Breuer (2000) highlights that ex-plicitly including off-balance-sheet positions pro-duces a more accurate measure of bank leverage. To assess leveraged positions in off-balance-sheet trans-actions resulting from a derivative contract, the basic derivative instruments—forwards and options—can be replicated by holding (and in the case of options, constantly adjusting) positions in the spot market of the underlying security, and by borrowing or lending in the money market. This replication of the contract maps the individual components into own-funds equivalents (equity) and borrowed-funds equivalents (debt), which can be used to measure the leverage contained in long and short forward positions and op-tion contracts. This on-balance-sheet asset equivalent of the exposure is also called the current notional amount. Overall leverage ratios, defined as on-balance-sheet assets plus off-balance-sheet exposures (gross or net), can be obtained following this method.

Summary Points

Indicators covered in this section suggest that two main measures are important for tracking capital ad-equacy: the ratio of regulatory capital to risk-weighted assets (the Basel capital adequacy ratio), and the ratio of capital to assets (the gearing ratio).

In countries where bank derivatives trading is con-sidered of systemic importance, it is also advisable, when monitoring capital ratios, to adjust for off-bal-ance-sheet items.

Asset Quality

Risks to the solvency of financial institutions most often derive from impairment of assets. This section looks at indicators that directly reflect the current state of bank credit portfolios,[29] including informa-tion on loan diversification, repayment performance and capacity to pay, and currency composition. Indi-cators of asset quality need to take into account credit risk assumed off-balance-sheet via guarantees, contingent lending arrangements, and derivatives—a subject covered at the end of the section. The quality of financial institutions' loan portfolios is also di-rectly dependent upon the financial health and prof-itability of the institutions' borrowers, especially the nonfinancial enterprise sector. Indicators of the fi-nancial strength of corporate and household borrow-ers are discussed in detail in Chapter IV.

The ratio of nonperforming loans (NPLs) to total loans is often used as a proxy for asset quality of a particular bank or financial system. Cortavarría, Dziobek, Kanaya, and Song (2000) note that in many countries, including most G-10 countries, as-sets are considered to be nonperforming when (1) principal or interest is due and unpaid for 90 days or more; or (2) interest payments equal to 90 days or more have been capitalized, refinanced, or rolled over. Some countries use forward-looking classifica-tion criteria, which focus on repayment capacity and cash flow of the borrower, and mirror more accu-rately the current economic value of a loan, therefore providing better quality indicators. For countries that are using the usual classification system, which in-cludes five categories: standard, special mention, substandard, doubtful, and loss, NPLs are often de-fined as loans in the three lowest categories. Never-theless, the classification criteria vary across coun-tries; hence, available measures of NPLs are not always comparable across countries and not even over time. In addition, some countries count only the unpaid portion of the loan, rather than the entire loan, as nonperforming. Meaningful cross-country comparisons of national NPL figures would require a common definition of NPLs.

A notion of asset quality geared toward the capac-ity of a bank to withstand stress should also consider the level of provisions. Provisions can be general—

---

[29]Credit (assets for which the counterparty incurs debt liabili-ties) is a more comprehensive concept than loans, and includes loans, securities other than shares (e.g., bonds), and miscella-neous receivables.

for possible losses not yet identified—or specific—for identified losses (loan-loss reserves). The definition and rules concerning general and specific provisions vary across countries, although standardized levels seem to gravitate toward 20 percent, 50 percent, and 100 percent for substandard, doubtful, and loss categories.[30] In some countries banks are also required to hold a general provision, sometimes calculated as 1 percent of standard-quality loans. The coverage ratio—the ratio of provisions to NPLs—provides a measure of the share of bad loans for which funds have already been set aside. An important indicator of the capacity of bank capital to withstand NPL-related losses is the ratio of NPLs *net* of provisions to capital.[31]

In situations of systemic banking distress, figures on restructured loans (and loan recoveries) are used as indicators of progress with NPL management. Trends in NPLs should be looked at in conjunction with information on recovery rates—for example, using the ratio of cash recoveries to total NPLs. Such information points to the level of effort or the ability of financial institutions to cope with high NPL portfolios.

Lack of diversification in the loan portfolio signals an important vulnerability of the financial system. Loan concentration in a specific economic sector or activity (measured as a share of total loans) makes banks vulnerable to adverse developments in that sector or activity. This is particularly true for exposures to the real estate sector (see Chapter IV). Country- or region-specific circumstances often determine the particular sectors of the economy that need to be monitored for macroprudential purposes.

Exposure to country risk can also be important in countries that are actively participating in the international financial markets. Data on the geographical distribution of loans and credit allow the monitoring of credit risk arising from exposures to particular (groups of) countries, and an assessment of the impact of adverse events in these countries on the domestic financial system through contagion.

Concentration of credit risk in a small number of borrowers may also result from connected lending and large exposures. Monitoring of connected lending is particularly important in the presence of mixed-activity conglomerates in which industrial firms control financial institutions.[32] Credit standards may be relaxed for loans to affiliates, even when loan terms are market-based. Connected lending can be measured against capital; the definition of what constitutes a connected party is usually set in consideration of the legal and ownership structures prevalent in a particular country. Consequently, this indicator is often difficult to use in cross-country comparisons.

The assessment of large exposures, usually calculated as a share of capital, aims at capturing the potential negative effect on a financial institution if a single borrower experiences difficulties in servicing its obligations.[33] Baldwin and Kourelis (forthcoming) note that it is important to monitor this indicator at the level not only of individual banks and the aggregate financial sector, but also of financial groups. If a number of affiliates have dealings with the same borrower, the group's credit risk exposure could well be underestimated if taken on a solo basis. Moreover, members of a group may sell loans to affiliated entities in advance of a periodic reporting in order to obscure their true exposure.

In countries where domestic lending in foreign currency is permitted, it is important to monitor the ratio of foreign currency-denominated loans to total loans. Delgado, Kanda, Mitchell Casselle, and Morales (2000) note that, ideally, a measure of risk from domestic lending in foreign currency should identify loans to unhedged domestic borrowers. In these cases, hedging would also include "natural hedges," or borrowings for which the adverse exchange rate impact on domestic currency obligations is compensated by a positive impact on revenue and profitability. The level of this ratio is related to that of foreign currency-denominated deposits to total deposits, although differences may be observed, notably when sources of foreign currency financing are available from lines of credit and other capital inflows. Hence, foreign currency loans should also be monitored as a share of foreign currency deposits and other foreign currency funding. Notably, however, because of the compound nature of credit and currency risk in foreign exchange-denominated lending, even institutions with a balanced foreign exchange position face risks when engaging in this type of lending.

Impact of Off-Balance-Sheet Operations

Monitoring bank soundness requires tracking the risks involved in off-balance-sheet operations (via guarantees, contingent lending arrangements, and de-

---

[30]Collateral could be taken into account in establishing provisions and a conservative value of the collateral could be deducted from the loan amount.

[31]The accounting treatment of provisions must be considered when looking at NPL ratios. As indicated above, in most G-10 countries, local accounting and prudential standards require banks to deduct specific provisions from loans, which adjusts the value of loans in response to changes in quality. In these cases, NPLs should be measured as a percentage of gross, rather than net, loans.

[32]See Baldwin and Kourelis (forthcoming).

[33]Exposure refers to one or more loans to the same individual or economic group. There is no standard definition of "large." In some countries, it refers to exposures exceeding 10 percent of regulatory capital.

rivative positions). As a general rule, FSIs should be calculated using "exposures"—that is, positions that are both on- and off-balance-sheet—rather than merely positions on the balance sheets. However, financial derivatives and off-balance-sheet positions present special problems in evaluating the condition of financial institutions because of the lack of reporting of positions in some countries, inadequate counterparty disclosure, high volatility, and the potential for spill-over effects. Such concerns have led the accounting profession to move toward explicit recognition of virtually all derivatives on balance sheets using a market value or equivalent measure of value (e.g., using delta-based equivalents).[34] International standards have also been proposed for the recognition, valuation, and disclosure of information on derivatives.[35]

Derivatives and, in particular, OTC derivatives, can contribute to the buildup of vulnerabilities and should be explicitly monitored. Although the institutions that intermediate the bulk of transactions in OTC derivatives markets are a limited number of large internationally active institutions (including commercial banks), smaller-scale interbank and interdealer activity account for a significant share of daily turnover.[36] This is because of the low cost and flexibility of OTC derivatives, which makes them efficient vehicles for position taking and hedging. Data on notional amounts of OTC derivatives transactions are common indicators in this area.

Summary Points

Indicators highlighted in this section as important in assessing bank asset quality include NPLs to total loans, NPLs net of provisions to capital, sectoral distribution of loans to total loans, connected lending to capital, large exposures to capital, and, where applicable, foreign currency-denominated loans to total loans. Ideally, indicators should be constructed using figures for "exposures" (on- and off-balance-sheet) rather than just loans.

Earnings and Profitability

Accounting data on bank margins, income, and expenses are widely used indicators of bank profitability. Common operating ratios are net income to average total assets—also known as return on assets (ROA)—and net income to average equity—also known as return on equity (ROE).[37]

Vittas (1991) notes that three types of operating ratios may be used in analyzing the performance of banks: operating asset ratios, operating income ratios, and operating equity ratios. The first relates all incomes and expenses to average total assets, the second to gross income, and the third to average equity. A summary of terms used in income statements can be found in Table 3.1.

Differences in capital structure, business mix, and accounting practices across countries, among individual banks, and over time must be considered in analyzing bank performance, and highlight the need to look at several operating ratios simultaneously. Differences in capital structure refer to differences in bank leverage. Banks with lower leverage (higher equity) will generally report higher operating asset ratios (such as ROA), but lower operating equity ratios. Hence, an analysis of profitability based on operating equity ratios (such as ROE) disregards the greater risks normally associated with high leverage. Operating income ratios may also be affected by leverage; notably, the interest margin and net income ratios will be higher, while the noninterest income and noninterest expenses ratios will be lower for banks with lower leverage (higher equity). The reason for this is that banks with higher equity need to borrow less to support a given level of assets and thus have lower interest expenses, which results in higher net interest and net income.

Differences in business mix derive from differing combinations of high- and low-margin business—for example, retail banking, which is associated with higher lending rates, lower deposit rates, and higher operating costs, and wholesale corporate banking. In this case, an analysis based on interest margins and gross income only may be misleading, since two banks may show wide differences in these ratios and still have equal ROA and ROE. Such an analysis disregards the fact that high margin business involves high operating costs. In the same vein, banks that offer a wider range of services, such as investment banks, will have much higher operating costs but also higher noninterest income.

Accounting practices that distort operating ratios cover such issues as the valuation (and revaluation, in the presence of inflation) of assets, the treatment of reserves for depreciation, employees' pensions, loan-loss provisions, and the use of hidden reserves. The possible impact of these factors must be taken into account in interpreting the ratios.

---

[34]The delta-normal method uses the linear derivative to approximate the change in portfolio value and the normal distribution as the underlying statistical model of asset returns.

[35]See Basel Committee on Banking Supervision and International Organization of Securities Commissions (1998).

[36]Schinasi, Craig, Drees, and Kramer (2000) report that in 1998 contracts between the major players accounted for roughly one-half of notional principal in interest rate derivatives and one-third in foreign exchange derivatives.

[37]The ratios can be calculated with various income measures—for example, before or after provisions and before or after tax charges and (net) extraordinary items.

Table 3.1. Income Summary

```
  + Interest income
  − Interest expenses
= Interest margin (net interest income)
  + Noninterest income
= Gross income
  − Noninterest expenses
= Net income
```

Returns can also be calculated on a risk-adjusted basis. The risk-adjusted return discounts cash flows according to their volatility: the more volatile the cash flow, the higher the discount rate and the lower the risk-adjusted return. Risk-adjusted return on capital (RAROC) states the return on capital required to offset losses on the underlying asset should volatility cause its value to decline (by two or more standard deviations). RAROC is particularly useful to banks in evaluating businesses and products according to their place along a risk/return spectrum, so as to correctly price a transaction and manage the risk-adjusted return. At the individual transaction level, RAROC is calculated as the ratio of interest margin associated with the operation (e.g., a loan) to loan value multiplied by the potential loss. At the aggregate level, it can be computed as interest margin to assets multiplied by the potential loss. Estimating the potential loss requires data on historical default and recovery rates and banks' ability to liquidate the assets (liquidity risk).

Summary Points

Relying too heavily on just a few indicators of bank profitability can be misleading. While ROA, ROE, and interest margin (and noninterest expenses) to gross income remain the key measures, they should ideally be supplemented by the analysis of other operating ratios.

Liquidity

The level of liquidity influences the ability of a banking system to withstand shocks. Common measures of liquidity include liquid assets to total assets (liquid asset ratio), liquid assets to short-term liabilities, or loans to assets as a crude measure.[38] The defin-

ition of liquid assets differs across countries but, in general terms, it refers to cash and its equivalents—any asset that is readily convertible to cash without significant loss. These indicators reflect the maturity structure of the asset portfolio and can highlight excessive maturity mismatches and a need for more careful liquidity management. Loan to deposit ratios (excluding interbank deposits) are also sometimes used to detect problems—a high ratio indicating potential liquidity stress in the banking system. These ratios may also reflect loss of depositor and investor confidence in the long-term viability of the institutions.

Information on the volatility of bank liabilities can supplement the information provided by liquidity ratios. Dziobek, Hobbs, and Marston (2000) propose a funding volatility ratio calculated as volatile liabilities minus liquid assets to illiquid assets (total assets minus liquid assets). A positive ratio indicates risk, since volatile liabilities are not fully covered by liquid assets. In practice, however, there are problems in applying this ratio, since it is difficult to know which assets should be classified as liquid and which liabilities should be classified as volatile.[39] More generally, bank liabilities that are subject to the risk of reversal of capital flows, such as external credit lines and deposits of nonresidents, should be monitored closely—for instance, through indicators of the size of this type of funding in total bank liabilities. Such indicators of exposure to international capital movements reflect the relevance of macroprudential analysis for assessments of external vulnerability.

As bank liquidity depends on the level of liquidity of the overall system, it is important to monitor measures of market liquidity. The focus may be on the treasury bill or central bank bill market, or on other markets that are most relevant to the liquidity of bank assets. Market liquidity can be captured by indicators of the tightness, depth, and resilience of a market.[40] Tightness indicates the general cost incurred in a transaction irrespective of the level of market prices and can be measured by the bid-ask spread (the difference between prices at which a market participant is willing to buy and sell a security). Depth denotes the volume of trades possible without affecting prevailing market prices and is proxied by the turnover ratio.[41] Resilience refers to

---

[38]Indicators of the maturity structure should distinguish between domestic and foreign liabilities and indicate the currency denomination of the liabilities.

[39]The need to further develop broad principles for quantifying funding liquidity risk was recently highlighted by the Multidisciplinary Working Group on Enhanced Disclosure of the Financial Stability Forum. See Financial Stability Forum (2001).

[40]See Committee on the Global Financial System (1999). Notably, in times of particular financial distress, dealers may not be willing to make a market at all in certain securities. Such instances can be captured through surveys of primary security dealers. See Nelson and Passmore (2001).

[41]The turnover ratio is the ratio of the average trading volume over a given period of time to the outstanding volume of securities.

the speed at which price fluctuations resulting from trades are dissipated; while there is still no consensus on an appropriate measure, one approach is to examine the speed of the restoration of normal market conditions after trades.

Where foreign currency transactions are relevant, liquidity management can be complicated if the availability of foreign currency is limited and interbank foreign exchange lines are vulnerable to disruption. In these cases, it is also important to measure the liquidity of foreign exchange markets and monitor its determinants. Foreign exchange liquidity will also depend on developments in the external sector, which is subject to the risk of reversal of capital flows (see above) or to the adequacy of foreign exchange reserves. More generally, sectoral balance sheet developments—such as in some indicator of reserve adequacy or corporate liquidity—could indicate buildup of liquidity stress in the same or other sectors.[42]

Standing central bank facilities, which are accessed at the initiative of banks, provide liquidity to banks (usually against collateral) and are an essential component of the liquidity infrastructure. On the other hand, a large increase in central bank credit to banks and other financial institutions—as a proportion of their capital or their liabilities—often reflects severe liquidity (and frequently also solvency) problems in the financial system. Jácome and Madrid (forthcoming) point out that beyond the traditional lender-of-last-resort role of the central bank, which is supposed to address limited liquidity problems, monetary authorities often get involved in banking crisis resolution because they are the most important (if not the only) source of large funds immediately available.[43] This participation usually implies providing liquidity support beyond best practices, injecting capital resources (in cash or bonds) to distressed institutions, and financing debt rescheduling and relief to the corporate sector. Monitoring central bank lending to financial institutions, therefore, can be important. Notably, however, these types of support are not always easily identifiable in central banks' financial statements, limiting the potential usefulness of this indicator to recognize banking liquidity (and solvency) problems.[44]

The dispersion in interbank rates is a highly relevant indicator of liquidity problems and bank distress. Very often, banks themselves first detect problems as they are exposed, or potentially exposed, to troubled institutions in the interbank market. High dispersion in interbank rates—measured, for instance, by the spread between highest and lowest rates in the market—may signal that some institutions are perceived as risky by their peers. As supplying banks can control their interbank positions through price and quantitative controls, high-risk institutions may be forced to engage in aggressive bidding for deposits. Changes in interbank credit limits or an unwillingness of some institutions to lend to others may indicate serious concerns.

Summary Points

Although liquid assets to total assets (the liquid asset ratio) and liquid assets to liquid liabilities remain the main indicators of bank liquidity, this section shows that "indirect" measures are also important and should be regularly monitored. These include indicators of systemic liquidity, such as bid-ask spreads and turnover ratios, central bank lending to deposit-taking institutions, and the dispersion in interbank rates (measured by the highest-to-lowest rate spread).

Sensitivity to Market Risk[45]

Banks are increasingly involved in diversified operations, all of which involve one or more aspects of market risk. In general, the most relevant components of market risk are interest rate and exchange rate risk. Moreover, in some countries, banks are allowed to engage in proprietary trading in stock markets, which results in equity price risk. Bank exposure to commodity price risk derived from the volatility of commodity prices varies significantly among countries, but is generally relatively small. Interest rate, exchange rate, equity price, and commodity price risks can be assessed by calculating net open positions according to the methodology proposed by the Basel Committee.[46] Measures of sensitivity to market risk would include the following:

• The duration of assets and liabilities is generally considered an accurate indicator of sensitivity to interest rate risk.[47] The greater the du-

---

[42]See Box 4.1 for further discussion of sectoral balance sheet analysis.

[43]Moreover, governments may feel tempted to shift to central banks the cost of bank resolution, at least partially, so as to hide these costs within the central bank balance sheet.

[44]Such transactions may also have important implications for the conduct of monetary policy and the financial position of the central bank, as described in Jácome and Madrid (forthcoming).

[45]See Chapter V for a discussion of the stress tests that are used in measuring sensitivity to market risk.

[46]See Basel Committee (1997, 1998).

[47]Duration is the weighted average life of an asset or liability (the weights being the present value of each cash flow as a percentage of the price of the asset or liability). Duration adjusts maturity to account for the size and timing of payments between now and maturity (e.g., the duration of a zero-coupon bond is equal to its maturity). In general, duration rises with maturity, falls with the frequency of coupon payments, and falls as the yield rises. The greater the duration of a bond, the greater is its volatility. For working purposes, duration can be defined as the approximate percentage change in price for a 1 percent change in yield. A discussion of the duration model can be found in Chapter V.

ration or "average" life mismatch between assets and liabilities, the greater is the risk. Alternatively, the average repricing period can be used to assess interest rate risk. The average repricing period refers to the average time to repricing for floating rate instruments and the remaining time to maturity for fixed rate instruments.

- The most common measure of foreign exchange exposure is the net open position. According to the Basel Committee on Banking Supervision, a bank's net open position in each currency should be calculated as the sum of the net spot position, the net forward position, guarantees, net future income and expenses not yet accrued but already fully hedged, the net delta-based equivalent of the total book of foreign currency options, and any other item representing a profit or loss in foreign currencies, depending on accounting conventions.

- The starting point for measuring a bank's equity risk exposure is its net open position in each equity. Equity derivative positions must be converted into notional equity positions (e.g., using delta-based equivalents).[48]

- Indicators of commodity price risk can be constructed that are similar to those for equity risk by looking at the absolute size of the investment in each commodity.

Summary Points

This section highlights some of the indicators and analytical methods used to measure sensitivity to market risk. Important indicators include the duration of assets and liabilities, and net open positions in foreign currencies and equities.

---

[48]For details on the methodology, see Basel Committee (1998).

IV   Other Sectors and Markets

Indicators of the health of financial systems should not simply look at the banking sector. Experience shows that risks to financial system stability can derive from developments in nonbank financial intermediaries (NBFIs), the corporate sector, households, and real estate markets.

Nonbank Financial Intermediaries

The presence and growth of NBFIs has raised macroeconomic and prudential issues, most recently during the Asian crisis. NBFIs—finance companies, collective investment schemes, insurance companies, and others—can build up substantial vulnerabilities and risks that often go undetected, partly owing to nontransparent disclosure practices and inadequate oversight. The collapse of NBFIs during the Asian turmoil (e.g., in Korea and Thailand) contributed directly or indirectly to a systemic crisis in the financial system. Accordingly, there is a need for a better awareness of the role of NBFIs in financial system stability and better monitoring of their condition.[49]

NBFIs' Behavior and Vulnerabilities

In many advanced countries, NBFIs already play a large enough role in the financial system to be considered systemically important, while elsewhere their rapid growth implies that they may be systemically important in the near future. NBFIs and banks often have ownership and investment linkages that make each subsector vulnerable to adverse developments in the other. Loss of consumer and investor confidence in NBFIs, even when their size remains relatively unimportant, can potentially undermine confidence in the entire system. Moreover, the systemic risks arising from a particular class of NBFIs—the highly leveraged financial institutions—were highlighted by

market turmoil following the near-failure of a large hedge fund in 1998. The size and growth in the operations of NBFIs raises a number of issues relating to the overall structure and functioning of financial systems, and thus have implications for financial system stability as well as for monetary and exchange rate policy.

NBFIs are typically not subject to the same prudential requirements as banks. Lower (or no) capital adequacy requirements increase NBFIs' vulnerability in the event of a shock. In addition, differential treatment may produce regulatory arbitrage and cause NBFIs to grow at the expense of banks, thus potentially increasing the vulnerability of the system (since NBFIs may potentially invest in riskier projects without the commensurate increase in necessary provisions and reserves). Preferential prudential treatment also decreases NBFIs' cost of funds and potentially allows them to offer higher funding rates than banks, hence attracting funds away from banks.

Competition between banks and nonbanks on the liability side is of particular concern when NBFIs can issue short-term financial instruments that can rapidly convert liabilities into means of payment. The existence of such quasi-deposits affects monetary operations since it may lead to an underestimation of money demand and a change in the money multiplier, thus reducing the effectiveness of reserve requirements as a monetary policy instrument and complicating monetary programming.[50]

The lending and funding operations of NBFIs can have an impact on a country's external debt, reserves, and exchange rate if they are carried out in foreign currency on a significant scale. Similarly, in financial systems with relatively thin foreign ex-

---

[49]A related issue, which is not explicitly covered in this paper, is that of offshore financial centers and the risks involved in the operations of these centers through links to domestic financial systems. See, for instance, IMF (2000e).

[50]In many countries, due to the nature of the instruments issued by NBFIs, their liabilities are not included in the narrow monetary aggregates (M1 and M2), which typically include the transferable deposit liabilities of the banking sector (mostly commercial banks). The liabilities of NBFIs are often included in wider monetary aggregates (M3 and M4), or are not included in monetary aggregates at all. In countries with substantial nonbank quasi-deposits, the wider monetary aggregates (M3 and M4) need to be monitored for monetary policy purposes. See IMF (2000f).

change and securities markets, the transactions of collective investment schemes, hedge funds, or securities firms can have a significant impact on the reserves, exchange rate, and securities prices. The buildup or liquidation of large positions can lead to high volatility in financial markets. Thus, indicators of gross and net positions of NBFIs in foreign exchange and securities may be important depending on the size of the positions relative to the overall market.

Indicators for Nonbank Financial Intermediaries

The development of specific FSIs for the NBFI sector would help to monitor, and raise awareness of, potential risks emanating from this sector. Such indicators should include the size of the NBFI sector—NBFI assets to total financial assets—to determine its systemic importance. The size threshold in terms of systemic importance would vary from country to country depending on the institutional setting, such as the manner in which NBFIs raise funds from the public (and from which segments of the public—small savers or wholesale investors). One way to measure relative importance would be to look at the liability side, and especially quasi-deposit liabilities, which are arguably more "systemically sensitive." The use of indicators such as NBFI assets to GDP is also revealing. Rapid expansion of credit and accumulation of assets in general, and in the NBFI sector in particular, may indicate the potential for problems in this sector. Accordingly, indicators of the growth in credit would be important. Another indicator of possible problems relates to overexpansion (and therefore unhealthy competition), which could be signaled by the growth in the number of NBFIs as well as by declining profit margins and/or capital.

Specific FSIs for the NBFI sector—resulting from the aggregation of balance sheet and income statement data by type of institution—would be useful in helping to gauge the health of NBFIs and detect the existence of potential risks. However, work on NBFIs is at an earlier stage than that on banks and more needs to be done to identify FSIs for the sector.[51] These indicators could include capital to asset ratios (to measure gearing and capital cushion) or

risk-weighted equivalents if available. Balance sheet or intermediation risk ratios could include liquid asset ratios and sector concentration ratios (to detect exposure to real estate or industrial sectors). NBFIs can be active in international markets or engage in foreign currency lending, making net foreign exchange exposure to capital another important indicator. Finally, the sustainability of the sector might be gauged by returns on equity and assets, and other operating ratios. Although to some extent similar to those used for banks, such indicators would need to pay due attention to the balance sheet and income characteristics of each subcomponent of the sector—such as finance (and leasing) companies, securities firms, collective investment schemes, and insurance companies. In the case of finance companies, for instance, indicators need to be adjusted to the basic characteristics of receivables (including off-balance-sheet risks) and the mix of funding sources. In the case of insurance, the indicators need to capture the specificity of each insurance market (i.e., health, life, property/casualty, and reinsurance).

Summary Points

Recent experience confirms the NBFIs' potential systemic role and the need to monitor their health and vulnerabilities. Data availability remains a key constraint in this area. Information about the NBFI sector—notably the unregulated entities—is generally difficult to obtain, assemble, and aggregate in a way that is consistent and comparable across countries. Although indicators exist that can capture the size and importance of NBFIs in the economy, more research and analysis is needed to develop a set of FSIs that captures the specificities of these intermediaries.

Corporate Sector

The quality of financial institutions' loan portfolios is directly dependent upon the financial health and profitability of the institutions' borrowers, especially the nonfinancial enterprise sector. The key role played by the corporate sector in recent episodes of financial sector distress is a reminder of the importance of monitoring developments in this sector. This section reviews recent literature on firms' characteristics and behavior that may increase the probability of crises. It also reviews evidence in support of the selection of specific FSIs for the corporate sector.

Corporate Behavior and Vulnerability

Recent theoretical and empirical work on the corporate sector and financial distress has looked at how firms respond to macroeconomic shocks, and

---

[51]The Financial Stability Forum recently recommended disclosure of a series of indicators for securities firms, insurance companies, and leveraged investment funds, in addition to banks. These included indicators of market risk, funding liquidity risk, and credit risk, as well as information of the nonlife insurance sector. These indicators are aimed at disclosure at the individual institution level. The Forum recognizes the need for further development of risk assessment concepts and methods in this area. See Financial Stability Forum (2001).

Table 4.1. Determinants of Corporate Vulnerabilities

	Financial Accelerator Models[1]				Collateral Models[1]	
	BG(95)	K(99)	KS(99)	GGN(00)	KM(97)	CK(00)
Structural vulnerabilities						
Access to nonbank financing	X					
Corporate governance						X
Legal infrastructure						X
Macroeconomic shocks						
Interest rate changes	X			X		X
Exchange rates changes				X		
Capital flows/liquidity		X	X			X
Domestic demand		X		X		
Terms of trade		X				X
Deflation			X	X		
Productivity					X	
Corporate sector indicators						
Leverage	X	X	X	X	X	X
Foreign debt		X	X	X		
Short-term or floating-rate debt	X		X			
Liquid assets	X					
Marketable collateral	X		X		X	X
Asset prices	X		X	X	X	X
Current cash flow	X		X			
Dividends			X			
Banking indicators[2]						
Availability of credit	X					X
Cost of credit	X					

[1]BG: Bernanke and Gertler; K: Krugman; KS: Kim and Stone; KM: Kiyotaki and Moore; CK: Caballero and Krishnamurthy; GGN: Gertler, Gilchrist and Natalucci.

[2]Some studies look specifically at bank vulnerabilities (capital adequacy and liquidity), which would feed into corporate vulnerability through the channels of availability (rationing) and cost of bank credit.

how this response in turn affects financing and investment decisions of the corporate sector and, through those decisions, the macroeconomy. The variables identified in some of this work are listed in Table 4.1. Much of this literature has focused on two aspects that are key to ensuring the repayment of corporate obligations: corporate net worth and cash flow, and marketable collateral. The "financial accelerator" approach stresses the role of microeconomic rigidities that occur due to informational asymmetries, where corporate net worth plays the role of collateral and helps to overcome incentive problems in lending. In these studies, macroeconomic shocks affect the real sector through corporate balance sheet effects.[52] The "collateral" approach stresses macroeconomic rigidities in the form of underdeveloped domestic financial markets and lack of internationally acceptable collateral. In these studies, crisis susceptibility is due to a shortfall in collateral needed to get domestic and foreign financing.[53]

Through the two channels of corporate balance sheets and collateral, the corporate sector is exposed to shocks such as a fall in asset prices, an increase in interest rates, or a slowdown in growth. Levels of corporate leverage influence the ability of firms to withstand these shocks, as empirically documented in a recent study by Kim and Stone (1999). The more leveraged and the less liquid the corporate sector, the more vulnerable it is to shocks. Large corporate debts denominated in foreign currency also make firms vulnerable to real devaluations, which affect their net worth and can render the economy financially fragile.[54]

[52]See for instance Bernanke and Gertler (1995), Krugman (1999), Kim and Stone (1999), and Gertler, Gilchrist, and Natalucci (2000). For a review of this literature, see Stone and Weeks (2001).

[53]See for instance Kiyotaki and Moore (1997), and Caballero and Krishnamurthy (2000).

[54]Céspedes, Chang, and Velasco (2000).

Prolonged distress in the corporate sector negatively affects firms' repayment capacity and creditworthiness, and results in a worsening of bank asset quality and ultimately higher NPLs. Gray (1999) examines how NPLs directly link corporate sector vulnerability to financial sector vulnerability. In his model, reduced corporate equity as a result of macroeconomic shocks results in an increase in NPLs, with the size of the increase depending on the composition of corporate debt (i.e., the importance of nonbank-financed debt). Nonpayments may be triggered by illiquidity, insolvency, or a collapse in credit culture in situations of systemic distress—a behavior known as "strategic defaulting." Since banks often book NPLs *after* a period (often three months) of nonpayment, direct indicators of corporate health such as cash flow adequacy can be more timely indicators of banking problems than NPL figures.

More recent IMF efforts in this area point to a strong link between macroeconomic developments and corporate leverage, and between corporate leverage and the probability and intensity of financial crises.[55] Stone and Weeks (2001) analyze the financial crises of the 1990s by dividing them into two stages: pre- and post-crisis equilibria. The first stage is a long buildup of balance sheet stress rooted in poor corporate governance, financial deepening, accelerated capital inflows, and, in many cases, overheating of the economy. These tensions leave the economy susceptible to financial shocks. A shock—usually external—triggers a sudden crisis, or a shift from a stable equilibrium into a new contractionary equilibrium. Empirical results show that both corporate leverage and aggressive bank lending can be significant indicators of the *probability* of a crisis. Corporate leverage, the availability of nonbank financing, and the legal environment are key elements in determining the *intensity* of crises. This has clear policy implications—the need to pay attention to corporate sector balances as well as to the breadth and quality of the domestic financial system.

Corporate Indicators

The literature reviewed above points to the importance of specific balance sheet and cash flow information—notably, data on leverage, interest cover, liquidity, and profitability—as indicators of corporate sector soundness. Recent studies have examined specific measures of corporate vulnerability, as summarized in Table 4.2. The table also includes indicators from a review of corporate rating methodologies.[56]

Excessive corporate leverage increases the vulnerability of corporate entities in the event of a shock and may impair their repayment capacity. A known indicator is total debt to equity, also called the gearing (or leverage) ratio. In general, indicators of corporate leverage can have total debt, total liabilities, or total long-term debt as the numerator; and equity, capital (defined as debt plus equity), or assets as the denominator.

Standard and Poor's (2000) discusses the limitations of some of these indicators. First, traditional measures focusing on long-term debt have lost much of their significance since companies rely increasingly on short-term borrowing. Second, the ratios suffer from difficulties in estimating the true economic value of assets.[57] Third, off-balance-sheet items should be factored into the analysis of leverage, such as operating leases, guarantees, contingent liabilities, and securitization (e.g., of accounts receivable). Fourth, the type of equity matters. For instance, many preferred stock issues have characteristics that make them quasi-debt in nature—such as fixed redemption dates, fixed dividend requirements, and (on occasion) higher redemption values. Fifth, broad indicators such as the ratio of total liabilities to total assets do not provide a good measure of risk of default, but are rather a proxy of what is left for the shareholders in case of liquidation. Sixth, corporate debt-equity ratios depend on countries' legal and accounting definitions of debt and equity, and are not easily comparable across countries.

Profitability is a critical determinant of corporate strength, affecting capital growth, attraction of equity, operating capacity, ability to withstand adverse events, and, ultimately, repayment capacity and survival. Sharp declines in corporate sector profitability—for example, as a result of economic deceleration—may serve as a leading indicator of financial system distress. Care should be taken to identify cyclical movements in corporate sector profitability, however. The most significant measures of profitability include (1) return on equity (earnings before interest and tax (EBIT) to average equity); (2) return on assets (EBIT to average assets); and (3) operating income to sales (EBIT to sales). Although the absolute levels of these ratios are important, it is equally important to focus on trends. Moreover, profitability information is particularly affected by market structure—that is, industry characteristics,

---

[55]There is a vast literature on the determinants of corporate leverage and its relevance to probability of financial distress and corporate credit ratings. See Rajan and Zingales (1995).

[56]See Fitch IBCA (1998), and Standard and Poor's (2000).

[57]Methods to mark asset values to market can be used, although they have shortcomings even at the individual firm level, and are hardly feasible at the aggregate level. Similarly, market values of equity are sometimes used, but these also have shortcomings as stock prices have a short-term bias, are correlated to alternative investment opportunities and are highly volatile, and may ultimately not reflect a company's ability to service its debt.

Table 4.2. Indicators for the Corporate Sector[1]

	BPS (00)	SW (01)	Fitch	S&P
Leverage				
Total liabilities to equity			X	
Total debt to total assets		X		
Total debt to equity			X	
Total debt to capital				X
Long-term debt to equity				
Total debt to market value of equity	X			X
Total debt plus off-balance-sheet liabilities to capital plus off-balance-sheet liabilities				X
Profitability				
Return on equity				X
Return on assets			X	
Operating income to sales			X	X
Cash flow adequacy				
EBIT to interest expenses			X	X
EBITDA to interest expenses				X
Debt payback period			X	
Liquidity				
Current ratio			X	
Quick ratio				

[1]BPS: Barnhill, Papapanagiotou and Schumacher; SW: Stone and Weeks; Fitch: Fitch IBCA; S&P: Standard and Poor's.

competitive environment, and pricing flexibility—implying that the analysis of these indicators would be best performed at the subsectoral level.

Earnings are also viewed in relation to a company's burden of fixed charges. Cash flow adequacy is often measured by the coverage ratio—earnings to interest expenses (interest payable less interest capitalized).[58] Earnings can be measured before interest and taxes (EBIT); or before interest, taxes, depreciation, and amortization (EBITDA).[59] This ratio measures the risk that a firm may not be able to make the promised fixed payments on its debts, and can reflect the closeness to corporate financial distress bet-

ter than corporate leverage. In addition to the interest coverage, other measures are often considered important, such as the debt payback period (total debt to discretionary cash flow). All these ratios are particularly critical in the analysis of corporate financial strength in distress situations.[60] A description of the main cash flow items is contained in Table 4.3.

Corporate liquidity determines the sector's ability to carry out business without endangering credit quality. Liquidity ratios include: (1) the current ratio—current assets (cash and accounts receivables) to current liabilities (debt and other liabilities coming due within a year); and (2) the quick ratio or acid test—current assets minus inventories to current liabilities. Notably, the current ratio is influenced by inventory valuation methods, which make international comparison particularly problematic.

Assessments of corporate sector vulnerability should also measure the ratio of corporate foreign currency debt to total debt, since significant currency depreciation could put severe pressure on those

[58]Interest expenses should be calculated to include leasing costs. Ideally, earnings should be adjusted to arrive at cash flow available for operations (e.g., by amending for noncash provisions and contingency reserves, asset write-downs that do not affect cash, and blocked funds overseas). See Moody's (1998).

[59]A recent study by Moody's (2000) concludes that the use of EBITDA interest coverage ratios can be misleading, notably as they (1) overstate cash flow in periods of working capital growth; (2) can be manipulated through aggressive accounting policies; (3) do not consider the amount of required reinvestment; and (4) say nothing about the quality of earnings. EBITDA, however, remains a legitimate tool for analyzing poorly performing corporations.

[60]Ratios such as funds flow from operations to total debt (and other off-balance-sheet liabilities) are more meaningful in assessing long-term profitability trends of corporate entities and sectors.

Table 4.3. Cash Flow Summary

Funds flow from operations

  + (–) Decrease (increase) in noncash current assets

  – (+) Decrease (increase) in nondebt current liabilities

= Operating cash flow

  – Capital expenditure

= Free operating cash flow

  – Cash dividends

= Discretionary cash flow

  – Acquisitions

  + Asset disposals

  + (–) Other sources (uses) of cash

= Prefinancing cash flow

Source: Standard and Poor's (2000).

---

banks whose clients have large foreign exchange debt-servicing burdens. This applies to both firms borrowing domestically in foreign currency and firms turning to foreign forms of financing.[61] Similarly, the ratio of foreign liabilities to foreign assets of the corporate sector may also be useful as foreign currency debt that is not matched with foreign currency earnings also increases the vulnerability of the corporate sector.[62]

Despite the growing theoretical and empirical literature on the subject, aggregate corporate sector balance sheet and income data remain limited at best, in quantity and timeliness—a fact that in itself limits the scope of research. As regards quantity, the data are usually available—at the disaggregated level—for listed companies only. This may bias the sample significantly, although the direction of this bias is theoretically ambiguous, and empirically it is likely to differ from market to market. As regards data quality, accounting quality determines the extent to which the picture determined by corporations' accounts, individually or at the aggregate level, can be relied upon as an accurate and comparable indicator of corporate strengths and weaknesses. Accounting quality can be assessed by looking at a country's accounting policies, including consolidation principles, income recognition rules, valuation (including inventory pricing) and depreciation methods, and goodwill treatment.

Summary Points

A number of key indicators of corporate soundness emerge from this section. They include total debt to equity as a measure of leverage; EBIT to average equity as a measure of return on equity; EBIT to interest and principal payments as a measure of debt-service coverage; and corporate foreign currency debt to foreign current assets as a measure of vulnerability to foreign exchange risk. Measures of liquidity, such as the current and quick ratios, can also be useful in assessing corporate vulnerabilities.

Household Sector

Although banks are often more exposed to companies than to households, the size of the exposure to the latter can be substantial, particularly in the most advanced economies. Furthermore, household consumption behavior has a strong effect on banks' main credit customers—the corporate sector—and household asset allocation decisions can impact bank liabilities and asset prices. This section reviews the literature on linkages between the household sector and financial intermediaries and markets, and discusses recent approaches to monitoring household developments that are relevant for the assessment of financial system soundness.

Household Behavior and Vulnerability

Two types of models are most relevant for explaining the linkages between households and the financial system—those that analyze household saving and borrowing decisions and those that explain their asset allocation.[63]

Household consumption and saving decisions are influenced by the availability of bank credit. There is an extensive empirical literature on the importance of current disposable income and household debt to future consumption. A recent study by Murphy (1998) finds that in the United States the ratio of debt service to income is a statistically significant predictor of future consumer spending and income growth: a high debt-service ratio sustained over several quarters precedes reductions in the rate of growth of consumption and income (although with an elasticity of significantly less than one). He argues that this can be explained by a reduction in bank lending in response to

---

[61]In some cases, strengthened financial sector supervision may create relative incentives for firms to borrow abroad, thereby shifting foreign exchange exposure-related vulnerabilities to the corporate sector.

[62]In the case of foreign exchange (as well as interest rate) exposures, swaps, caps, and hedges are tools that can significantly affect corporate financial positions.

[63]Household consumption patterns can also be a leading indicator of corporate and financial sector distress. For example, there is some evidence that consumers react at an early stage to macroeconomic shocks such as higher interest rates, notably in their demand for housing and consumer durables. See Bernanke and Gertler (1995).

a rise in household debt burden that directly affects consumption (especially of durable goods) and indirectly affects income growth. Empirical evidence on this point, however, is not conclusive.[64]

Financial institutions typically react to changes in macro and household financial variables (such as earnings, collateral, and debt levels) by restricting access to credit if these variables signal changes in the borrowers' capacity to repay their obligations. Liquidity constraints may affect the composition of household balance sheets, especially the leveraged purchases of consumer durables and residential housing, and the preference for liquid assets. This, in turn, may affect the corporate sector—as household consumption has a large impact on domestic output, and household participation in the equity market may affect the ability of firms to raise funds for investment. Thus, banks are exposed to households directly, through their repayment capacity on consumer and mortgage loans, as well as indirectly, through the effect that household consumption decisions have on corporate sector financial strength.

Banks are also exposed to households through the liabilities side of their portfolios. The decision to deposit savings in financial institutions is part of the portfolio allocation behavior of households, which is a function of the supply and demand of assets based on current wealth, and of households' risk propensity.[65] Household deposits typically provide banks with the most stable and low-cost source of funding. Since, in principle, these funds may be withdrawn rapidly, the stability of household deposits is very important given the often substantial maturity gap that arises from banks' intermediation function (i.e., channeling short-term savings into longer-term investment). Stability is a function of the confidence that households have in the individual institutions and the financial system as a whole. Although direct measures of consumer confidence in the financial sector are difficult to identify, indirect measures that focus on bank liquidity are available, such as changes in the level or volatility of savings deposits or changes in the interest rates paid.[66]

Household Indicators

The vulnerability of households may be assessed through the use of sectoral balance sheets, flow of

funds, and other macro and microeconomic data. Table 4.4 presents indicators used and approaches taken by three central banks in monitoring developments in the household sector. These indicators tend to follow from the variables highlighted by the literature as important: wealth, current income, debt, and asset prices. Indicators include debt to GDP or to assets, and debt burden (principal and interest payments) to disposable income. Some of the other indicators used follow from credit risk analysis (see Chapter V), such as the ratio of debt to collateral value (or loan-to-value ratio), which is important for mortgage loans.

Most of the analysis of the vulnerability of the household sector is primarily focused on direct bank exposure and thus relies heavily on debt-servicing capacity. However, the other indicators on asset composition highlight the concern that households may be significantly exposed to equity and real estate price movements.

One potentially useful approach in looking at the linkages between households, firms, financial institutions, and the macroeconomy at the empirical level is that of using national sectoral balance sheets (see Box 4.1). Sectoral balance sheets permit the examination of a comprehensive set of linkages between households, firms, financial institutions, the public sector, and the rest of the world, and can potentially help to better understand the complex interactions among these sectors. This approach, however, is limited by data availability.

Summary Points

Due to the direct and indirect exposure of financial institutions to the household sector, indicators of household financial strengths and vulnerabilities are important in assessing financial institutions' soundness and resilience to shocks. Key indicators of financial strength of the household sector include household indebtedness to GDP and household debt burden to income. These indicators should be complemented with detailed data on financial institutions' credit outstanding to the household sector.

Real Estate Markets

In many countries, unbalanced real estate developments have contributed to financial sector distress. Notwithstanding their importance from a macroprudential standpoint, analyses of developments in the real estate markets are rarely undertaken on a systematic basis. This section presents some evidence on the link between macroeconomic developments

---

[64]For instance, a recent paper by De Ruiter and Smant (1999) finds that in the Netherlands high debt ratios do not slow durables consumption.

[65]In particular, portfolio diversification reduces risks to household income. This underscores the need to monitor the composition of household balance sheets, not just net wealth, to better gauge vulnerabilities.

[66]For a discussion of bank liquidity indicators, see Chapter III.

Table 4.4. Household Indicators Used in Norway, Sweden, and the United Kingdom

---

Norway

National accounts and financial market data
   Wage income and disposable income trends
   Savings trends
   Interest expenses to cash income
   Interest expenses to interest income excluding interest on insurance claims
   Gross loan debt to disposable income
   Gross loan debt to gross claims excluding insurance claims
   Gross loan debt to value of housing wealth
   Composition of financial assets (deposits, securities, and equities)
   Composition of interest-bearing debt
   Net investment in financial assets to disposable income trends

Micro data
   Interest and debt burdens classified by age, socioeconomic conditions (e.g., employment status), and income categories

Sweden

Risk buildup indicators
   Lending to households by category of financial institution
   Lending by type of credit
   Lending by income decile
   Housing prices
   Employment and income
   Stock prices

Repayment ability indicators
   Wages, real disposable income, and wealth
   Interest cost after tax to disposable income
   Household debt to disposable income

United Kingdom

Leverage indicators
   Total and mortgage interest payments to personal disposable income
   Total lending (debt stock) to the household sector to residential and financial wealth
   Secured and unsecured debt to residential and financial wealth
   Net financial wealth
   Real household income

Financial distress indicators
   Personal bankruptcies
   Mortgages in arrears to total mortgages

Potential threat indicators
   Housing prices, including asset bubbles as measured by the ratio of housing prices to earnings
   Interest rate changes
   Unemployment

Source: Begum, Khamis, and Wajid (forthcoming).

---

and real estate prices and between the real estate sectors and financial sector soundness.

Macro-Financial Linkages

Rapid increases in real estate prices—often fueled by expansionary monetary policies or by large capital inflows—followed by a sharp economic downturn can have a detrimental impact on financial sector profitability and health, by affecting credit quality and the value of collateral. The literature on real estate market developments can be categorized into three groups: papers that explain how real estate mar-

kets function in normal circumstances, those that focus on the emergence of price bubbles, and those that study the (over)exposure of the financial system to risky real estate loans.

In well-functioning markets, the price formation process should equilibrate supply and demand, and the fundamental equilibrium price would be the price at which the existing stock of real estate equals replacement costs.[67] If the price of real estate is above (below) the replacement cost, construction

---

[67]Di Pasquale and Wheaton (1996).

Box 4.1. Sectoral Balance Sheet Analysis[1]

Sectoral balance sheet analysis is potentially useful in assessing vulnerabilities in the financial system from stresses elsewhere in the economy. Balance sheet analysis uses sectoral breakdowns in the national accounts for the following sectors: households, nonfinancial corporations, nonbank financial institutions, banking institutions, the government, and the rest of the world. In addition to identifying the specific asset/liability components that may be particularly vulnerable to fluctuations in asset prices, interest rates, and income flows, the balance sheets of all sectors taken together can help to clarify the linkages among sectors that could transmit financial disturbances. A useful, albeit partial, framework for such analysis is provided by the flow of funds accounts.[2]

A number of countries have started to utilize sectoral balance sheet data in their assessments of financial stability. The approach used combines macro, micro, and sometimes a market view of the sectors, focusing on the risk posed to the banking sector by the enterprise and household sectors. The macro approach uses sectoral balance sheet and flow of funds data including loan growth to enterprises, enterprise debt and interest rate burdens, sectoral trends in enterprise profits, profit margins and dividend payments, debt and interest burdens of households, financial wealth of households, and real income of households.

Although there is some merit in using sectoral balance sheets to form judgments about buildup of financial stress in some sectors and their implications for other sectors, there are also important limitations. Specifically, transactions based on balance sheet data are unlikely to provide an accurate picture of asset price movements and would not capture off-balance-sheet items. A more robust analysis should be grounded in a comprehensive macro model specifying the behavioral features of assets markets and deriving sectoral balance sheets consistent with the flows and prices determined by the model.

More generally, the usefulness of this approach is constrained by the very limited availability of data. In the UN system of national accounts, sectoral balance sheet data are available only for two industrialized countries. Flow data on capital finance accounts by sector exist for only 15 countries (of which 12 are industrialized), either from UN or OECD sources. Information on sectoral balance sheets from national sources is limited, and generally focused on banks and other financial institutions.[3]

---

[1]This box is based on Begum, Khamis, and Wajid (forthcoming).

[2]Flow of funds accounts link savings and investment in the national accounts with their associated lending and borrowing activities. Because they provide information on changes in assets and liabilities, these accounts are an important complement to balance sheet data.

[3]As part of the IMF's ongoing work to facilitate the implementation of internationally agreed statistical standards, the *Quarterly National Accounts Manual* provides guidance to countries in the compilation of national accounts. See Bloem (2001).

will increase (decrease) until the market regains equilibrium—that is, the adjustment of stock of real estate takes place in the construction sector. An increase in the number of investors, the existence of optimistic investors, an increase in the number of office workers, or other similar events can trigger an outward shift of the demand curve, and the new equilibrium will move to a higher level. In well-functioning markets, real estate cycles will be driven by normal economic cycles, due to the changes in expected growth in income, real interest rates, taxes, future demographic profile, etc.[68]

Growth in construction in excess of income growth and other fundamentals may be related to price bubbles that develop from credit booms. A number of mechanisms can trigger or amplify the appearance of cycles and bubbles in real estate markets, some due to nonfinancial characteristics of real estate markets,

others due to the lending behavior of banks.[69] These include (1) fixed supply and the behavior of investors willing to purchase property in periods of rising prices; (2) construction time lags in the adjustment of property supply to increasing demand; (3) the impact of rising real estate prices on loan collateral values; (4) moral hazard in the form of over-guaranteed and under-regulated financial institutions, leading to risky behavior and high investment and asset prices; (5) increased competition for financing risky real estate projects subsequent to financial liberalization; (6) rising real estate prices resulting in greater lending to

---

[68]IMF (2000a), in particular Chapter III on "Asset Prices and the Business Cycle."

[69]Real estate markets are characterized by heterogeneity, consisting of a series of geographical and sectoral submarkets that lack a central trading market. No two properties are identical and information on market transactions is often limited and not generally available. Also, real estate markets are typically characterized by infrequent trades, a negotiated pricing process, large transaction costs, and very rigid supply. In contrast to stock markets and other financial markets there is, therefore, no clear market price.

the real estate sector, as a bank's own holdings of real estate—hence its capital—increase in value.

The arguments above suggest that the higher the exposure of banks to real estate, the more amplified the cycles in real estate markets. Still, banks seem to underestimate the risks associated with high exposure to this sector due to the following factors:

- *Disaster myopia or low frequency of shocks*: Real estate cycles are often long and a whole generation may have passed since the last severe downturn in prices. During a boom period, profitability in terms of (expected) returns is high and the risks are underestimated.

- *Inadequate data and weak analysis*: Even under the best circumstances, it may be difficult to estimate the present value of a real estate project. It will depend, among other things, on projected rents, discount rates, anticipated inflation, loss in value due to depreciation, and vacancies due to the development of competing projects. In many countries, data on building permits, new construction contracts, rents, market prices, and vacancy rates are not readily available or are difficult to obtain and verify.

- *Perverse incentives or moral hazard* resulting from a combination of highly leveraged real estate developers and asymmetric information may lead to bank financing of real estate projects that are riskier than if they were financed largely through equity—as developers will initiate riskier projects when they can shift most of the downside risk to banks. This is more likely to occur in economies with highly leveraged banks, poorly designed financial safety nets and weak supervision, and/or weak corporate governance.

Empirical analysis so far on the link between real estate market developments and banking distress has been limited. A recent IMF study reviews the experience of 13 cases of extreme price swings in the real estate market associated with increased banking sector vulnerability.[70] The authors find a strong correlation between real estate price developments and credit growth: real estate booms are generally preceded or accompanied by a boom in banking credit to the private sector, and busts by a strong contraction of credit growth. This supports the notion that the availability of financial resources is one of the driving forces of prices in this market.

The empirical results also show that in most of the cases studied, real estate prices surged sharply and began falling prior to the beginning of financial dis-

tress.[71] On average, residential real estate prices corrected for inflation rose by more than 20 percent from seven to two years before the beginning of financial distress; then fell by more than 15 percent two years prior to the beginning of financial distress; and then continued to fall at least until the peak of the crisis. A similar pattern can be observed for commercial property prices in most countries for which there are data. For the few cases where data on stock prices of real estate companies are available, there is a tendency for these prices to fall drastically before a banking crisis and to bottom out or stabilize by the onset of crisis. A logit-probit analysis of episodes of banking distress and real estate price developments confirms that a downturn in residential real estate prices increases the probability of banking distress.[72]

Case studies highlight the role that shocks to output and monetary conditions, combined with weak capital positions of banks, can play in increasing the vulnerability of the financial system to real estate market price swings. However, the lack of high frequency data on real estate markets and poor data on credit exposure (and NPLs) to the real estate sector for most of the countries has so far prevented more thorough analyses.

Real Estate Indicators

Ideally, a range of indicators should be analyzed to get a sense of real estate market developments (demand, supply, prices, and links to the business cycle) and to assess financial sector exposure to the real estate sector (Table 4.5).

To determine bank exposure to the real estate sector, it is important to have information on the size of the credit exposure and its riskiness. To accomplish the latter, it may be necessary to distinguish between different types of real estate-related loans, which may have very different risk characteristics. For example, it would be useful to distinguish between lending: (1) for the purpose of investment in (purchase of) commercial real estate; (2) for the purpose of investment in residential real estate, including mortgages; (3) for the purpose of real estate construction or, more generally, lending to construction companies; and (4) collateralized by real estate. The degree of risk involved could be estimated by the average probability of default as well as the default recovery rate for the different types of debt, as in Barnhill, Papapanagiotou, and Schumacher (2000).[73] A

---

[70]Hilbers, Lei, and Zacho (2001).

[71]Cross-country comparisons of real estate developments, however, are complicated by differences among countries in financing structure, tax structure, and the use of real estate as collateral.

[72]Commercial real estate prices were not analyzed due to the scarcity of data.

[73]See Chapter V for details.

Table 4.5. Real Estate Indicators

Indicator	Definition and measurement issues
Prices	
Real estate price index	In equilibrium, price would equal cost; thus, this price index can be compared to the construction cost index to assess the incentive to build. Subindices that reflect developments in subsectors (commercial, industrial, and residential) or geographical areas are also useful in assessing exposure to real estate.
Construction cost index	This index could proxy for fundamental prices under certain conditions; however, market imperfections and inclusion of other nonconstruction costs in the index often drive replacement costs away from fundamental prices.
Rents	In principle, the present discounted value of future rents should equal the price of the property. However, the path of rents may be difficult to predict and rents may include other services, such as utilities, which drive the discounted value of today's rents away from fundamental prices.
Land prices	Since land is in fixed supply, speculation will be reflected in rapidly rising land prices at rates higher than construction costs. Thus, land prices could be indicators of the development of bubbles.
Supply and demand	
Property stock available	Current supply of property.
Vacancy or occupancy rates	Gap between demand and supply.
Number/value of new buildings	Additions to current supply.
Number/value of sales	Indication of current demand. In particular, the number and value of sales in a given period divided by the stock of supply at the beginning of the period provides an indicator of the tightness of the market.
Stock price indices	The stock price of real estate firms should equal the present discounted value of profits; changes in the index could signal changing perceptions on sector profitability.
Exposure to the real estate sector	
Loans outstanding	While this may give a broad indicator of exposure, different types of real estate loans (e.g., residential mortgages, commercial mortgages, loans to construction companies, other loans collateralized by real estate) may have different characteristics.
Loan-to-value ratio	This ratio is an important indicator of the probability of default.
NPLs	This indicator could act as a proxy for the expected default rate.

critical aspect of this analysis is the ratio of loan to value (where value is equal to market value of equity for firms, and to housing value for mortgages and collateralized loans). Default is likely to occur when the loan to value ratio exceeds a threshold that can be estimated from historical series. An alternative would be to use the NPL ratio as the expected default rate for the different types of loans.

A major obstacle to in-depth analyses of real estate markets is the availability of data, in particular for emerging markets. No major international database provides data on real estate prices or other indicators of developments in real estate markets. The Bank for International Settlements (BIS) maintains a small database with annual residential and commercial property prices for 17 industrialized countries, but only part of the data is publicly available. In some advanced and emerging markets, real estate

indicators are available from commercial sources, generally focusing on the largest cities and covering prices (sales and rentals) as well as current and forecast supply, demand, and vacancy rates. Sectoral breakdowns cover industrial, commercial, retail, and residential space. These data are heterogeneous: differences exist with respect to timeliness, assets considered, quality, and coverage.[74] Finally, financial sector data on the exposure of the financial system to real estate markets are also difficult to obtain,

---

[74]In particular, some commercial property indices cover only offices, while others include retail property as well as property used for production and storage. There are also technical differences, such as the weights used to combine different localities and qualities of property, as well as whether the mean or the median price in the sample is chosen.

and the quality and definition of such indicators vary significantly.

Summary Points

A number of key indicators of financial institutions' exposure to real estate markets emerge from this section. They include the loans outstanding to the real estate sector to total loans, possibly supple-mented by data on nonperforming loans to the sector (as a share of total real estate loans). The usefulness of these data, however, is often limited by the fact that different types of real estate-related loans have very different risk characteristics. In addition, it is important to monitor developments in real estate markets, particularly with regard to prices, for both residential and commercial real estate.

V Stress Testing of Financial Systems

Having discussed specific FSIs, it is important to look at methods to analyze them. A variety of methods are available to analysts to derive from FSIs conclusions about the stability of financial systems—from simple ratio analyses to more complex macro and microeconomic modeling. The focus of this chapter is on one particular method—stress testing—originally developed as a bank risk management tool, but the object of growing interest for its potential application to analyses of strengths and vulnerabilities at the level of the system as an aggregate, as opposed to the individual institutions.

Defining System-Wide Stress Tests

Stress testing is a key element of macroprudential analysis that helps to monitor and anticipate potential vulnerabilities in the financial system. It adds a dynamic element to the analysis of FSIs—that is, the sensitivity, or probability distribution, of FSI outcomes in response to a variety of (macroeconomic) shocks and scenarios.[75] By anticipating the potential impact of specified events on selected FSIs, stress tests also help to focus on financial system vulnerabilities arising from particular banking system, macroeconomic, and sectoral shocks.

Stress testing, as used in the context of assessments of financial system stability, is a generic term that refers to a range of statistical techniques. Stress testing measures are used to help to identify (1) risk exposures in individual financial institutions; and (2) system-wide risk exposures that potentially have systemic consequences for the financial system.

Stress testing is a process encompassing a variety of techniques that include:

- *Sensitivity analysis*, which seeks to identify the exposures and likely elasticity of responses of financial institutions to relevant economic variables, such as interest rates, exchange rates, equity prices, etc.
- *Scenario analysis*, which seeks to assess the resilience of financial institutions and the financial system to an exceptional but plausible economic scenario.
- *Contagion analysis*, which seeks to take account in a stressful situation of the implications of transmission of shocks from individual financial exposures to potential vulnerabilities in the financial system as a whole.

System-wide stress testing methodologies derive from stress tests conducted at the individual institution level. As a result, there are similarities, but also important differences, between the two techniques. Individual portfolio stress tests aim at assisting in managing risks within a financial institution and ensuring the optimal allocation of capital across risk-taking activities.[76] A good stress test needs to be relevant to the current portfolio, include all relevant market rates, encompass potential regime shifts and market illiquidity, and consider the interaction of different risks. Specification issues include (1) the type of risk or risks to be considered and appropriate models to be used; (2) the range of factors to be considered—a single factor sensitivity test or the simultaneous movement in a group of risk factors as in scenario analysis; (3) the specification of the type of shock (i.e., whether the shock affects the level, volatilities, and/or correlation of prices), the size of the shock, and the time horizon; (4) the assets to be included; (5) whether to use historical prices, hypothetical prices, or Monte Carlo-simulated prices;[77]

---

[75]Commonly tested shocks include a slowdown in economic growth, balance of payments shocks, and changes in inflation, interest rates, and exchange rates. Equity and security price shocks may also be important, particularly in the most advanced countries where banks and bank borrowers have significant capital market exposures. It is important to identify shocks that are representative of past country experiences, or that are justified by observed volatilities and correlations in the data.

[76]The Committee on the Global Financial System (CGFS) has recently undertaken a global census of stress tests in use at major financial institutions. See CGFS (2000 and 2001).

[77]The Monte Carlo method is a stochastic technique that generates prices by performing repeated statistical sampling experiments from random numbers. It approximates the market's price-generating process.

Figure 5.1. Decision Sequence for Stress Testing

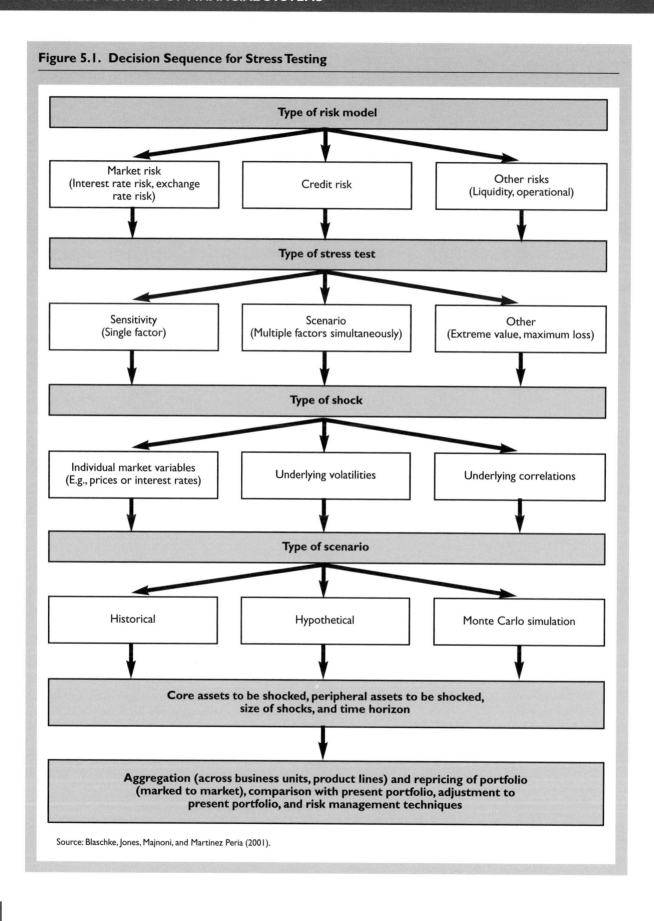

Source: Blaschke, Jones, Majnoni, and Martinez Peria (2001).

and (6) the aggregation (across business units and/or product lines) of the portfolio. Figure 5.1 provides a summary of these specification issues.

Aggregate stress tests are measures of the risk exposure of a group of institutions to a specified stress scenario. Their aim is to help to identify structural vulnerabilities and overall risk exposures in a financial system that could lead to the disruption of financial markets. The emphasis is on potential externalities and market failures. Aggregation of stress testing scenarios has the potential to expose the vulnerability of a system to simultaneous attempts by firms to reduce exposures—a cumulative effect on market liquidity usually not captured by individual portfolio stress tests. An FSAP stress test is not a simple extension of firm-specific stress test methodology: (1) there are direct links to macro imbalances, (2) the test looks at system-wide exposures, and (3) the measures must aggregate across product groups and financial intermediaries.

The type and range of FSIs used in stress tests depend on model specification. In simple models, the impact of changes in a macroeconomic variable (such as a slowdown in GDP, which increases credit risk) is measured in terms of resulting changes in the FSI capturing banks' exposure to that risk (such as nonperforming loan ratios). In more sophisticated models, the impact of shocks is measured in terms of changes in capital adequacy ratios. The channels through which shocks ultimately affect capital adequacy would usually involve indicators of bank sensitivity to market risks, asset quality and provisioning, liquidity, and profitability. The results of stress tests provide information on the elasticity of a given FSI to macroeconomic shocks, and such elasticity itself can be used as an indicator of bank vulnerability to individual risks or a combination of risk factors.

Stress testing of financial systems presents various methodological challenges. It is difficult to decide the scope of the test and to clearly delineate aggregate portfolios that are systemically important. In practice, (1) complex interlocking claims among financial institutions make it difficult to take aggregate net positions at face value (i.e., interbank claims may represent a small net aggregate position, but the gross positions may be systemically significant); (2) a narrow focus on "systemically important" institutions (e.g., banks, if nonbanks do not present a systemic threat) may be more manageable, but may overlook potential vulnerabilities; and (3) inclusion of foreign-owned banks requires information on the stability of the parent group.

Other challenges include aggregation issues and the choice of models. Aggregation of stress tests may be accomplished either by compiling the results of stress tests of individual portfolios—which may

not be comparable if the tests were conducted using different methodologies—or by applying a common stress test to an aggregated portfolio—which may suffer from less detailed knowledge of the individual institutions. Finally, while the aim of an aggregate stress test is to identify structural vulnerabilities (i.e., externalities and market failures), the tools for quantifying these effects in a simple measure are not yet well developed.[78] Bearing in mind these limitations, approaches do exist that can be used in conducting assessments of financial system soundness.[79] Data availability and the sophistication of the financial system largely determine the approach to be used in each country with respect to each relevant risk.

The Macro-Stress Test Linkage

The value added of a system-wide stress test comes from the coordination between an informed forward-looking macroeconomic perspective, a scope that covers all systemically important financial groups, and the ability to detect system-wide exposures. Hence, it is important to properly identify macroeconomic shocks and scenarios. Macro-financial linkages go two ways—shocks can have a negative impact on the health of debtors and creditors, which in turn can have an adverse impact on macroeconomic performance. Stress tests, however, focus on the former linkage: the impact of macroeconomic shocks on the health and stability of the financial system, and of the banking sector in particular.[80]

Several studies have analyzed the types of shocks or changes to the macroeconomic environment that may be important in increasing the vulnerability of financial systems. In the aftermath of the Asian crisis, a wave of financial sector studies confirmed that macroeconomic shocks to output, exports, prices and the terms of trade, asset price booms, and inappropriate monetary and exchange rate policies, all resulted in financial pressures and contributed to crises in financial systems that are inherently fragile.[81] More recently, Johnston, Chai, and Schumacher (2000) and Blaschke, Jones, Majnoni, and Martinez Peria (2001) identify a number of shocks that are typically considered when assessing financial systems' resilience using stress tests. These in-

---

[78]For instance, results from the most complex simulation techniques may be strongly model-dependent and sensitive to the parameter used.

[79]For a detailed discussion of these approaches, see Blaschke, Jones, Majnoni, and Martinez Peria (2001).

[80]In the presence of large, complex financial institutions with insurance activities, however, attention should also be paid to vulnerabilities arising from the nonbanking activities of the group.

[81]For a complete review of this literature, see Evans, Leone, Gill, and Hilbers (2000).

clude higher interest rates, foreign exchange devaluation, higher inflation, lower growth rates, and unfavorable changes in the terms of trade. Blaschke, Jones, Majnoni, and Martinez Peria (2001) review the experience of conducting stress tests in the context of the FSAP, and conclude that the impact of these types of macroeconomic shocks on the banking system can be significant.

- *Credit shocks.* Macroeconomic factors that help to explain the behavior of the NPL ratio include the real interest rate, the terms of trade, the exchange rate, GDP growth, and real estate prices. This evidence is based on a limited number of countries, however, and should be considered as a starting point in the analysis, rather than a definitive relationship.

- *Liquidity shocks.* Withdrawal of deposits or credit lines may cause a liquidity shock to financial institutions. Liquidity shocks may also be correlated to other shocks and indirectly affect bank liquidity. For example, during currency attacks, banks may face a liquidity crisis as depositors withdraw their funds from the banking system to purchase foreign currency. Hence, financial institutions may lose access to both domestic and foreign exchange funding during a currency crisis.

- *Interest rate shocks.* For interest rate risk, shocks may take the form of a parallel shift in the yield curve, a change in the slope of the yield curve, and a change in the spread between different interest rates with the same time horizon. These shocks typically affect the level of interest rates, but may also increase their volatility and correlation. Larger shocks may take place particularly in countries with illiquid money and capital markets as well as countries that are vulnerable to currency crises.

- *Exchange rate shocks.* Shocks to one or more exchange rates can affect financial institutions' soundness, depending on their type of exposure. Switches in currency regimes, capital account liberalization, increasing use of derivatives, changes in regulation and supervision, and the entry of foreign banks are all factors that can make a difference in how a financial system reacts to foreign exchange shocks. In countries where domestic lending in foreign currency is allowed, exchange rate fluctuations can have direct as well as indirect impacts, as some borrowers may be exposed to currency risk that translates into credit risk for the lender (see Chapter II).

- *Equity price shocks.* Particularly in the more advanced countries, banks have significant direct and indirect exposures to capital markets as a result of their own investment and trading portfolios and those of their borrowers. In addition, adverse developments in these markets can result in a marked general economic slowdown and, consequently, lead to deterioration in the credit quality of the loan book. Shocks related to adverse capital market developments can be measured by market-based indicators such as stock market prices and credit spreads.[82]

Measurement Techniques

Individual Risk Factor Assessments

Financial institutions face a number of risks—related to changes in credit quality, liquidity, interest rates, exchange rates, and equity and commodity prices. Stress tests typically consider these risks separately. The basic method in assessing the impact of each risk factor is to determine the exposure of the portfolio to each risk and then to estimate the change in the market value of the portfolio that may result from a change in the risk factor (i.e., the risk sensitivity of the net exposure). This may be relatively straightforward in the case of spot foreign exchange holdings, but more complex for holdings that are expected to deliver cash flows over time (e.g., bonds and loans). The following sections briefly describe the different techniques that can be useful in assessing individual risk factors.

Credit Risk

Credit risk is the risk of default of a counterparty or obligor on its contractual obligations (i.e., the risk that principal or interest on an asset may not be paid in full according to contractual agreements). Measuring the credit risk of a portfolio of instruments involves estimating the likelihood of default on each instrument,[83] the extent of losses in the event of default, and the likelihood that other obligors will default at the same time (i.e., the joint distribution or correlation of defaults).

Several estimation methods are available, including from commercial sources.[84] Most of these approaches, however, are microeconomic and have limitations in estimating the impact on the financial system of a common external shock and in detecting

---

[82]For examples of market-based indicators for the United States, see Nelson and Passmore (2001).

[83]For instance, the default mode approach uses an average default probability and the mark-to-market approach uses a default transition matrix based on the borrower's credit rating.

[84]Theses include J.P. Morgan's *Creditmetrics*, Credit Suisse's *CreditRisk+*, and KMV's *Credit Monitor Model*.

elements of systemic risk. A proper specification of the impact of macroeconomic factors on financial institutions would enable an analysis of different sources of credit risk in countries at different levels of economic development, of different sizes, and with different financial structures.

One approach that helps to assess the systemic impact of macroeconomic shocks is the *nonperforming loan (NPL) approach*.[85] It uses time series of NPLs for homogenous groups of banks or borrowers as the dependent variable in a regression using macroeconomic factors as independent variables—such as nominal interest rates, inflation, GDP growth, and terms of trade. The coefficients of the regression provide an estimate of the sensitivity of bank borrowers to the relevant macroeconomic and financial risk factors. This approach also permits dynamic analyses of short-run and long-run (equilibrium) effects—for instance, by using an error correction model. Assuming a linear risk exposure to the macroeconomic variable, an expression of the volatility of NPLs can be derived as a function of the volatilities of the macroeconomic variables and the unexplained volatility. A major shortcoming of this approach is the lack of long and reliable time series for NPLs, particularly for transition and developing countries that are experiencing structural changes.

Liquidity Risk

There are two types of liquidity risk: asset liquidity risk and funding liquidity risk. The former refers to the inability to sell assets at current market prices because of the size of the assets and the short amount of time available for liquidation (a situation commonly referred to as "fire sales"). The latter refers to the inability to access sufficient funds to meet payment obligations in a timely manner. Two main methods are available to assess liquidity risk: the sources and uses of funds approach and the structure of funds approach.

- *The sources and uses of funds approach* defines as liquidity gap the difference between the sources and uses of funds: a deficit occurs when uses of funds exceed sources. This method requires forecasting of uses and sources of funds in any given liquidity planning period.

- *The structure of funds approach* looks at the structure of the sources and uses of funds. Future liquidity requirements are forecast by dividing bank deposits and other sources of funds into categories based on their probability of being

withdrawn, and identifying the sources of funds that can become illiquid in certain situations.

Interest Rate and Other Market Risks

Interest rate risk is the risk of loss by a financial institution when the interest rate sensitivity of its assets and liabilities are mismatched. Simple methods such as *gap analysis*—including the repricing model, the maturity-gap model, and the duration model—can be used to assess this risk (see also Chapter III). Gap analysis requires the compilation of a maturity (or repricing) schedule for all assets and liabilities.[86] The "gap" is the difference in interest flows on the holdings of assets and liabilities in each time bucket, measured in terms of net assets for the repricing model. In the maturity gap and duration models, the "gap" is the difference in the maturity of assets and liabilities, measured in terms of weighted maturity for the maturity-gap model and average life for the duration model. In the simple repricing model, the value of assets and liabilities does not change with a change in interest rates, while in the more complex duration model the value of assets and liabilities changes according to the interest elasticity of each asset or liability. The duration model provides more accurate estimates of the change in the market value of a portfolio due to changes in interest rates.[87] However, its additional data requirements (i.e., the cash flow profile and expected change in the interest rate term structure) make it difficult to use in countries with less sophisticated statistical systems.

Exchange rate and equity price risks can be assessed by calculating net open positions (see Chapter III). *Exchange rate risk* is the risk that exchange rate changes will affect the value of an institution's assets and liabilities (both on- and off-balance-sheet), capital position, and income. *Equity price risk* is the risk that stock price changes will affect the value of an institution's portfolio. It has a specific and a general component. A risk is specific when it is associated with movements in the price of an individual stock. A risk is general when it is related to movements of the stock market as a whole. *Commodity price risk* refers to the potential losses that may result directly from changes in the market price of bank assets, liabilities, and off-balance-

---

[85]For details see Blaschke, Jones, Majnoni, and Martinez Peria (2001).

[86]For the simple repricing model, this requires the sorting of assets and liabilities according to their time to repricing for floating rate instruments, and remaining time to maturity for fixed rate instruments; net assets are then classified in a limited number of time categories or "buckets." For the duration model, it is necessary to know the timing of future cash flows, which may also be grouped into different buckets.

[87]See, for instance, Saunders (2000).

Table 5.1. Data Requirements for an Integrated VaR Analysis

Financial Environment

- Time series of short-term interest rates or credit spreads on loans of different quality, to undertake volatility and correlation analyses
- Specific estimates of the term structure of interest rates for each currency, and credit risk level at the date of the risk assessment
- Prices for a set of interest rate options for each currency

Portfolio Structure

- Asset/liability maturity mismatches that create interest rate risk
- Asset/liability currency mismatches that create foreign exchange risk
- Credit quality of governments, companies, and individuals to which the institution has loaned money and that affect the risk of adverse rating changes and default
- The level of geographic and economic sector concentration (diversification) in the asset portfolio that affects portfolio credit risk
- The level of seniority and security for the loans in the portfolio that substantially affects the recovery rates on loans that may default
- Off-balance-sheet transactions that either reduce (i.e., hedge) or increase the institution's risk level

Business Loans

- Each bank's business loan broken down, for each currency, by sector, credit quality, maturity, and yield
- Estimates of typical debt to value ratios for loans of various credit qualities broken down by sector
- Balance sheets, income statements, and credit classification for all large exposures
- Time series of default rates on business loans by credit quality one year (or up to five years) prior to default
- Estimates of loan default recovery rates by sector and seniority of loan

Mortgage Loans

- Number and amounts of real estate loans broken down by loan-to-value ratios
- Typical loan-to-value ratio at which mortgage loans default

Other Securities and Money Market Deposits

- Amounts of government securities, equity securities, etc., broken down for each currency by type, credit quality, maturity, and yield

---

Source: Barnhill, Papapanagiotou, and Schumacher (2000).

---

sheet instruments, as well as indirectly through the loan portfolio, due to commodity price changes. Even if financial institutions do not take positions in commodities or commodity-linked instruments directly, they may be subject to commodity price risk indirectly via the impact on their loan portfolios. This occurs if the borrowers' ability to repay their debt is affected by shocks to commodity prices. This indirect source of commodity risk can be particularly important for many banks in developing countries that lend to exporters and/or importers of commodities.

Value at Risk

The Value at Risk (VaR) framework is a multivariate approach to risk assessment that is used to capture multiple risks arising *under normal market cir-* *cumstances*. The VaR is an estimate of the maximum loss on a portfolio with a given probability over a preset horizon. It is used in financial institutions as a risk management tool to set limits to the amount of risk that is undertaken, typically, in the trading book. VaR techniques can complement stress tests in that the latter are used to measure risks arising at the tail-end of the distribution of market circumstances under which financial systems operate.

There are two broad approaches to estimating a VaR. The local valuation method uses an estimate of the sensitivity of the portfolio multiplied by the estimated price change to arrive at the estimated change in value of the portfolio. The full valuation approach recalculates the value of the portfolio using historical or Monte Carlo simulations of prices. The correlations and volatilities used for a VaR calculation can be based on historical or on implied observations.

VaR techniques are usually applied to the measurement of market risk, but they have also been used to assess credit risk. Barnhill, Papapanagiotou, and Schumacher (2000) attempt to measure banks' integrated market and credit risks using a full-valuation VaR in which the two types of risks are correlated. In their model, corporate credit risk is a function of leverage and the volatility of the firm's equity value. The paper simulates the financial environment as a probability distribution of 8,000 scenarios, where under each scenario, each bank client has a different debt to equity ratio. These simulated debt to equity ratios are then mapped into credit risk categories and the value of each client loan is discounted by the (simulated) interest rate that corresponds to the credit risk category under each scenario (Table 5.1). Their methodology provides a base for evaluating potential changes in a bank's asset/liability portfolio composition (e.g., credit quality, sectoral and geographic concentration, maturity structure, and currency composition) as well as its capital ratio.

VaR techniques have several limitations, however.[88] The VaR measure is not the maximum amount that a portfolio could lose; rather, it is a loss threshold that will be exceeded with only a small probability. VaR techniques can provide useful information to decision makers about the likely pattern of events that will influence the value of a portfolio, but they are less useful in providing information about unlikely events. In addition, the analysis is sensitive to the assumed distribution and underlying estimation techniques.[89] Data requirements for conducting VaR analyses are substantial, and the degree of detail required on individual positions makes it practical to apply this method to individual institutions only. In view of the variety of VaR techniques used in financial institutions, aggregating individual VaR results in a meaningful manner can be very difficult. For these reasons, the VaR framework is rarely used in conducting aggregate stability assessments.

[88]Blaschke, Jones, Majnoni, and Martinez Peria (2001).

[89]For example, the normal distribution is typically used, but if the true distribution has fatter tails, the VaR may underestimate possible losses. Moreover, linear approximations are commonly used to estimate changes in the value of the portfolio, but this may underestimate the VaR if movements in asset prices are large and the portfolio includes many assets with nonlinear payoffs (e.g., options).

Part II

Country Practices

VI The IMF Survey on FSIs

Introduction

The *Survey on the Use, Compilation, and Dissemination of Macroprudential Indicators*, conducted jointly in mid–2000 by the IMF's Monetary and Exchange Affairs Department and Statistics Department, has been an important step in the IMF's program to develop a common set of FSIs. The objective of the survey was to obtain information on national needs and practices related to FSIs in order to (1) gauge the usefulness of specific indicators; (2) assess compilation and dissemination practices in order to help identify international best practices where possible; (3) evaluate whether the Special Data Dissemination Standard (SDDS) or other vehicles could have a role in encouraging the public dissemination of FSIs; and (4) explore the analytical frameworks used by member countries in macroprudential analysis. The structure of the survey is described in Box 6.1.

Box 6.1. Structure of the Survey on FSIs

The survey had two parts (see Appendix V). The first part, the *User Questionnaire*, gathered information from financial supervisors, financial policy officials, and the private sector on the usefulness of the FSIs and methods of macroprudential analysis. The second part, the *Compilation and Dissemination Questionnaire*, inquired about national practices in compiling and disseminating FSIs.

The structure of the survey benefited from consultations with national authorities, international organizations, and the private sector.[1] These consultations also contributed importantly to improving the list of FSIs to be surveyed and to assessing their uses and potential reliability. The survey covered a total of 56 FSIs selected as representative of the work and focus of a broad range of users. The FSIs and their components were grouped into six major categories derived from the CAMELS framework used by bank supervisors to evaluate individual financial institutions. The six categories of FSIs included in the survey were:[2]

- *Capital adequacy;*
- *Asset quality (lending institutions);*
- *Asset quality (borrowing institutions);*
- *Profitability and competitiveness;*
- *Liquidity;* and
- *Sensitivity to market risks.*

The FSIs included in the survey largely focused on information about depository corporations (banks), but included some key information on their corporate and household counterparties (see Table 6.2). This focus was determined in light of the importance of banking institutions and the generally greater amount of information available for banks compared to other types of institutions. However, further research is needed on analyzing and quantifying the influence of the condition of nonbank financial institutions and financial markets on financial sector soundness.

Central banks in each economy received the survey, with a request that they coordinate its distribution, completion, and return to the IMF. They were asked to distribute the survey within their economies to whichever parties they judged could best provide representative information on needs and practices relating to FSIs. These parties included central government policy or analysis offices, supervisory agencies, and private sector participants.

The survey was made available in English, French, and Spanish, and was dispatched in early June 2000 to the IMF membership and several offshore financial center nonmembers. Copies were also sent to relevant international organizations. Responses were requested by the end of July 2000. Most responses were received during July and August 2000.

---

[1]Consultations on the design of the survey were held with the Asian Development Bank, the Bank for International Settlements, the Basel Committee on Banking Supervision, the Committee on the Global Financial System, the European Central Bank, the Financial Stability Forum, the International Association of Insurance Supervisors, the Organization of Economic Cooperation and Development, and the World Bank. Consultations were also held with central banks and supervisory offices in nine countries and with representatives from the private sector—commercial and investment banks, rating agencies, investment research firms, and real estate market research firms.

[2]The quality of management of financial institutions was not included in the survey because of concerns that quantitative measures of management would not be reliable.

Response to the Survey

The IMF received a total of 122 responses to the survey (74 percent of those receiving it), covering 142 countries and other jurisdictions. All of the 122 respondents completed the first part of the survey—the *User Questionnaire*, while 93 respondents completed the second part—the *Compilation and Dissemination Questionnaire*. The high response rate is an indication of the importance attached worldwide to issues relating to macroprudential analysis and the possible role of FSIs in such analysis. This view is bolstered by the effort made by respondents to answer the survey thoroughly and provide detailed comments. Table 6.1 shows a summary of the responses by type of economy.

Table 6.1 shows that the response was broadly based—all industrial economies responded to the survey, the response rate from emerging economies

was very high, and over half of all developing economies responded. The response rate of emerging and developing economies was lower for the *Compilation and Dissemination Questionnaire* than for the *User Questionnaire*, perhaps reflecting more limited programs than those in industrial countries to compile and disseminate FSIs.

Table 6.2 provides a summary of the responses by indicator. It shows the number of respondents compiling and disseminating each of the FSIs included in the survey, and users' evaluation of the usefulness of FSIs. The next two chapters will discuss these results in greater depth. Chapter VII will discuss users' evaluation and the usefulness ratings, while Chapter VIII will discuss country compilation and dissemination practices. The qualitative results of the survey will be discussed in Chapter IX. In addition to the tables and figures included in the text, Appendix IV provides detailed survey results.

Table 6.1. Summary of the Responses by Type of Economy[1]

	Worldwide		Industrial Economies		Emerging Economies[2]		Developing Economies	
	Number of responses	Percent of total sent survey	Number of responses	Percent of total sent survey	Number of responses	Percent of total sent survey	Number of responses	Percent of total sent survey
Total responses	122	74	24	100	53	88	45	56
Africa	24	60	—	—	4	100	20	56
Asia-Pacific	26	76	3	100	14	82	9	64
Europe	40	87	19	100	15	94	6	55
Middle East	6	43	—	—	5	71	1	14
Western Hemisphere	26	83	2	100	15	94	9	69

[1]Responses from regional central banks that covered their respective memberships are counted as a single response.
[2]There is no standard list of emerging economies. For the purposes of this paper, the group of emerging economies was based on the tables used in the May 2000 issue of the IMF's *World Economic Outlook*.

Table 6.2. Summary of the Responses by Indicator

FSI		Number Compiling FSIs	Number Disseminating FSIs	Average Usefulness Score
1. *Capital adequacy*				
1.1	Basel capital adequacy ratio	85	53	3.8
1.1a	Ratio of Basel tier I capital to risk-weighted assets	81	44	3.6
1.1b	Ratio of Basel tier I + tier II capital to risk-weighted assets	79	43	3.4
1.1c	Ratio of Basel tier I + II + III capital to risk-weighted assets	36	21	3.0
1.2	Distribution of capital adequacy ratios (number of institutions within specified capital adequacy ratio ranges)	21	11	3.3
1.3	Ratio of total on-balance-sheet assets to own funds	34	17	3.2
2. *Asset quality*				
(a)	Lending institutions			
2.1	Distribution of on-balance-sheet assets, by Basel risk-weight category	77	33	3.4
2.2	Ratio of total gross asset position in financial derivatives to own funds	15	5	2.8

Table 6.2 *(concluded)*

FSI		Number Compiling FSIs	Number Disseminating FSIs	Average Usefulness Score
2.3	Ratio of total gross liability position in financial derivatives to own funds	13	5	2.8
2.4	Distribution of loans, by sector	76	60	3.6
2.4a	*of which*: loans for investment in commercial real estate	41	30	3.2
2.4b	*of which*: loans for investment in residential real estate	51	40	3.2
2.5	Distribution of credit extended, by sector	46	35	3.5
2.6	Distribution of credit extended, by country or region	42	28	3.1
2.7	Ratio of credit to related entities to total credit	26	7	3.4
2.8	Ratio of total large loans to own funds	29	8	3.5
2.9	Ratio of gross nonperforming loans to total assets	42	28	3.9
2.10	Ratio of nonperforming loans net of provisions to total assets	39	22	3.8
(b)	Borrowing institutions			
2.11	Ratio of corporate debt to own funds ("debt-equity ratio")	17	9	3.4
2.12	Ratio of corporate profits to equity	15	9	3.3
2.13	Ratio of corporate debt-service costs to total corporate income	13	9	3.2
2.14	Corporate net foreign currency exposure	6	2	3.2
2.15	Ratio of household total debt to GDP	13	7	3.0
2.15a	*of which*: ratio of mortgage debt to GDP	25	16	2.8
2.15b	*of which*: ratio of household debt owed to depository corporations to GDP	29	23	2.9
2.16	Number of applications for protection from creditors	13	10	2.7
3. Profitability and competitiveness				
3.1	Rate of change in number of depository corporations	35	28	2.7
3.2	Ratio of profits to period-average assets (ROA)	42	29	3.6
3.3	Ratio of profits to period-average equity (ROE)	44	31	3.6
3.4	Ratio of net interest income to total income	39	23	3.5
3.5	Ratio of trading and foreign exchange gains/losses to total income	30	16	3.3
3.6	Ratio of operating costs to net interest income	38	21	3.4
3.7	Ratio of staff costs to operating costs	37	21	3.2
3.8	Spread between reference lending and deposit rates	25	16	3.5
3.9	Share of assets of the three largest depository corporations in total assets of depository corporations	35	16	2.9
4. Liquidity				
4.1	Distribution of three-month local currency interbank rates for different depository corporations	23	12	2.9
4.2	Average interbank bid-ask spread for three-month local currency deposits	18	11	2.9
4.3	Ratio of liquid assets to total assets	37	20	3.5
4.4	Ratio of liquid assets to liquid liabilities	37	22	3.6
4.5	Average maturity of assets	18	5	3.4
4.6	Average maturity of liabilities	18	5	3.4
4.7	Average daily turnover in the Treasury bill (or central bank bill) market	33	24	2.8
4.8	Average bid-ask spread in the Treasury bill (or central bank bill) market	25	14	2.8
4.9	Ratio of central bank credit to depository corporations to depository corporations' total liabilities	20	11	2.9
4.10	Ratio of customer deposits to total (noninterbank) loans	33	14	3.2
4.11	Ratio of customer foreign currency deposits to total (noninterbank) foreign currency loans	24	11	2.9
5. Sensitivity to market risk indicators				
5.1	Ratio of gross foreign currency assets to own funds	24	9	3.1
5.2	Ratio of net foreign currency position to own funds	25	11	3.4
5.3	Average interest rate repricing period for assets	17	4	3.0
5.4	Average interest rate repricing period for liabilities	16	3	3.0
5.5	Duration of assets	22	9	3.2
5.6	Duration of liabilities	21	7	3.2
5.7	Ratio of gross equity position to own funds	21	8	2.9
5.8	Ratio of net equity position to own funds	15	8	3.0
5.9	Ratio of gross position in commodities to own funds	7	2	2.4
5.10	Ratio of net position in commodities to own funds	8	3	2.4

VII Usefulness of FSIs

The first part of the survey, the *User Question-naire*, gathered information from three types of users of macroprudential information—financial supervisors, policy analysts within the central bank or government, and the private sector (mainly financial market participants, financial rating agencies, and academics)—regarding their needs for data. Users were asked to rate the usefulness of each FSI and the preferred periodicity and timeliness. The quantitative information on the usefulness of FSIs was supplemented by a series of open-ended questions about the analytic framework applied in each country, national research programs on FSIs, and special issues affecting macroprudential analysis.

Figure 7.1 presents respondents' average usefulness scores for the six major categories of FSIs, disaggregated by type of economy—industrial economies, emerging economies, and developing economies. The scale for scores is: 1—not useful, 2—sometimes useful, 3—useful, and 4—very useful.

Respondents judged all major categories of FSIs to be broadly useful, with slightly more users in emerging countries deeming them useful than did other users.[90] Indicators of *capital adequacy*, *asset quality (lending institutions)*, and *profitability* were most widely deemed to be useful, followed by indicators of *liquidity* and *sensitivity to market risk*. Fewer users in industrial economies, in particular, deemed the *liquidity* and *sensitivity to market risk* indicators useful. Several industrial economy respondents commented that the *liquidity* and *sensitivity to market risk* indicators were sophisticated and possibly difficult to construct to achieve precise results.

FSIs by Usefulness Group

The FSIs are divided into four groups in Tables 7.1–7.3 based on their average usefulness scores for all respondents. Group I comprises the FSIs deemed very useful, as reflected in average usefulness scores

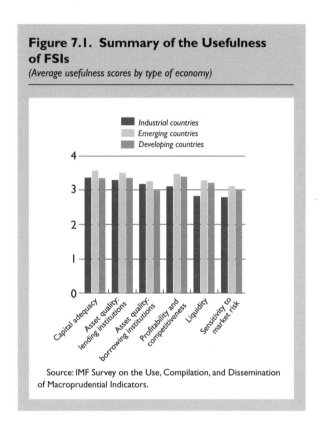

Figure 7.1. Summary of the Usefulness of FSIs
(Average usefulness scores by type of economy)

Source: IMF Survey on the Use, Compilation, and Dissemination of Macroprudential Indicators.

of 3.5 and above. Group II comprises FSIs deemed useful, with average scores of 3.0–3.4; Group III comprises moderately useful FSIs, with scores of 2.5–2.9; and Group IV comprises less useful FSIs, with scores of 2.4 and lower.

Very Useful FSIs

Table 7.1 presents the 13 FSIs with an average usefulness score of 3.5 or over. These FSIs include central elements of bank soundness: two of them—the Basel capital adequacy ratio and one of its components—relate to the capital base, which serves as a buffer to withstand shocks; while four of them measure profitability, which serves to sustain the capital

---

[90]Appendix IV, Table A4.3 provides a detailed matrix with usefulness scores for FSIs by type of user and type of economy.

Table 7.1. Group I FSIs by Type of Economy
(Very useful FSIs, with average usefulness ratings of 3.5 and higher)

FSI		All Countries	Industrial Countries	Emerging Countries	Developing Countries
1.1	Basel capital adequacy ratio	3.8	3.7	3.9	3.6
1.1a	Ratio of Basel tier I capital to risk-weighted assets	3.6	3.6	3.6	3.5
2.4	Distribution of loans, by sector	3.6	3.5	3.6	3.5
2.5	Distribution of credit extended, by sector	3.5	3.3	3.6	3.6
2.8	Ratio of total large loans to own funds	3.5	3.2	3.6	3.6
2.9	Ratio of gross nonperforming loans to total assets	3.9	3.9	3.9	3.8
2.10	Ratio of gross nonperforming loans net of provisions to total assets	3.8	3.8	3.8	3.8
3.2	Ratio of profits to period-average assets (ROA)	3.6	3.5	3.8	3.6
3.3	Ratio of profits to period-average equity (ROE)	3.6	3.5	3.8	3.6
3.4	Ratio of net interest income to total income	3.5	3.3	3.6	3.6
3.8	Spread between reference lending and deposit rates	3.5	3.4	3.6	3.5
4.3	Ratio of liquid assets to total assets	3.5	3.2	3.6	3.5
4.4	Ratio of liquid assets to liquid liabilities	3.6	3.2	3.7	3.7

base. The quality of banks' assets—as covered by data on nonperforming loans, the distribution of assets, and asset liquidity—comprise the remainder of the FSIs in Group I.

Useful FSIs

Table 7.2 presents the Group II FSIs, with average usefulness scores of 3.0 to 3.4. These FSIs cover some of the elements of capital adequacy, the distribution of bank credit by risk-weight category and by country, the financial conditions of the corporate and household sectors, some of the elements of operating income and expenses of banks, the maturity and duration of assets and liabilities, and other market risks. This is the largest group, comprising 27 FSIs or 48 percent of all FSIs surveyed.

The 40 indicators in Groups I and II represent a sizeable group of FSIs that have been judged useful for analyzing financial soundness, among which 13 were on average judged very useful. These FSIs cover all six categories of FSIs and comprise 71 percent of the indicators surveyed. Notably, users in emerging and developing countries generally marked the usefulness of these 40 indicators equal to or higher than those in industrial countries.[91]

In assessing FSIs in Groups I and II, the responses from supervisors, policy officials, and private sector respondents were broadly similar, although supervisors tended to rate the FSIs more useful than the other users did, and policy officials tended to assign greater usefulness to FSIs on the financial condition of the household sector (Appendix IV, Table A4.3).

Moderately Useful FSIs and Less Useful FSIs

Table 7.3 presents those FSIs with usefulness scores of 2.5–2.9 (Group III) and under 2.5 (Group IV). The Group III FSIs include several indicators related to asset quality and many of the liquidity indicators. In general, there is no clear break between the Group II and Group III FSIs—7 of the 14 Group III FSIs have borderline average scores of 2.9 and most have average scores of 3 or higher within at least one of the types of economy groupings.

Only two FSIs (the ratio of gross positions in commodities to own funds and the ratio of net position in commodities to own funds) are classified in Group IV. Many respondents indicated that banks in their countries are forbidden to hold commodity positions.

Additional FSIs Identified by Respondents

The *User Questionnaire* also asked respondents to identify FSIs they considered useful but were not covered in the survey. A relatively small number of additional FSIs were suggested. Appendix III provides a summary of respondents' suggestions.

---

[91]For example, among the Group II FSIs, six have average usefulness scores in emerging and developing countries that are markedly higher than those in industrial countries.

Table 7.2. Group II FSIs by Type of Economy
(Useful FSIs, with average usefulness ratings of 3.0 to 3.4)

FSI		All Countries	Industrial Countries	Emerging Countries	Developing Countries
1.1b	Ratio of Basel tier I + II capital to risk-weighted assets	3.4	3.2	3.6	3.4
1.1c	Ratio of Basel tier I + II + III capital to risk-weighted assets	3.0	2.9	3.1	3.1
1.2	Distribution of capital adequacy ratios (number of institutions within specified capital adequacy ratio ranges)	3.3	3.3	3.4	3.1
1.3	Ratio of total on-balance-sheet assets to own funds	3.2	2.9	3.3	3.3
2.1	Distribution of on-balance-sheet assets, by Basel risk-weight category	3.4	3.2	3.5	3.4
2.4a	Loans for investment in commercial real estate	3.2	3.3	3.3	3.1
2.4b	Loans for investment in residential real estate	3.2	3.3	3.2	3.2
2.6	Distribution of credit extended, by country or region	3.1	3.2	3.2	2.8
2.7	Ratio of credit to related entities to total credit	3.4	3.0	3.6	3.5
2.11	Ratio of corporate debt to own funds ("debt-equity ratio")	3.4	3.4	3.5	3.3
2.12	Ratio of corporate profits to equity	3.3	3.1	3.4	3.2
2.13	Ratio of corporate debt service costs to total corporate income	3.2	3.2	3.4	3.0
2.14	Corporate net foreign currency exposure	3.2	3.2	3.4	2.9
2.15	Ratio of household total debt to GDP	3.0	3.2	3.0	2.8
3.5	Ratio of trading and foreign exchange gains/losses to total income	3.3	3.2	3.4	3.3
3.6	Ratio of operating costs to net interest income	3.4	3.0	3.6	3.6
3.7	Ratio of staff costs to operating costs	3.2	2.8	3.4	3.4
4.5	Average maturity of assets	3.4	3.0	3.4	3.6
4.6	Average maturity of liabilities	3.4	3.0	3.4	3.6
4.10	Ratio of customer deposits to total (noninterbank) loans	3.2	2.9	3.3	3.3
5.1	Ratio of gross foreign currency assets to own funds	3.1	2.7	3.2	3.2
5.2	Ratio of net foreign currency position to own funds	3.4	3.1	3.6	3.5
5.3	Average interest rate repricing period for assets	3.0	2.8	3.3	3.0
5.4	Average interest rate repricing period for liabilities	3.0	2.8	3.2	3.0
5.5	Duration of assets	3.2	3.0	3.4	3.0
5.6	Duration of liabilities	3.2	3.0	3.3	3.0
5.8	Ratio of net equity position to own funds	3.0	2.8	3.0	3.1

The most frequently identified useful additional FSIs were asset prices. Among the asset prices suggested were the prices of real estate, both commercial and residential, and equity prices, including the stock prices of the depository corporations' subsector relative to the overall stock price index, and stock prices disaggregated by industry sectors. To prevent the masking of relevant information through

Table 7.3. Groups III–IV FSIs by Type of Economy
(Modestly useful and less useful FSIs, with average usefulness ratings of 2.5 to 2.9, and under 2.5, respectively)

FSI		All Countries	Industrial Countries	Emerging Countries	Developing Countries
Group III FSIs (average usefulness ratings of 2.5 to 2.9)					
2.2	Ratio of total gross asset position in financial derivatives to own funds	2.8	2.7	3.0	2.6
2.3	Ratio of total gross liability position in financial derivatives to own funds	2.8	2.7	2.9	2.6
2.15a	Ratio of household mortgage debt to GDP	2.8	3.1	2.8	2.7
2.15b	Ratio of household debt owed to depository corporations to GDP	2.9	3.0	2.8	2.8
2.16	Number of applications for protection from creditors	2.7	2.8	2.7	2.5
3.1	Rate of change in number of depository corporations	2.7	2.4	2.7	2.9
3.9	Share of assets of the three largest depository corporations in total assets of depository corporations	2.9	2.7	3.1	2.9
4.1	Distribution of three-month local-currency interbank rates for different depository corporations	2.9	2.7	3.1	2.8
4.2	Average interbank bid-ask spread for three-month local-currency deposits	2.9	2.9	3.0	2.7
4.7	Average daily turnover in the treasury bill (or central bank bill) market	2.8	2.3	3.0	3.1
4.8	Average bid-ask spread in the treasury bill (or central bank bill) market	2.8	2.3	3.0	3.0
4.9	Ratio of central bank credit to depository corporations to depository corporations' total liabilities	2.9	2.6	3.1	2.8
4.11	Ratio of customer foreign currency deposits to total (noninterbank) foreign currency loans	2.9	2.6	3.1	2.9
5.7	Ratio of gross equity position to own funds	2.9	2.8	3.0	3.0
Group IV FSIs (average usefulness ratings of 2.4 and lower)					
5.9	Ratio of gross position in commodities to own funds	2.4	2.3	2.5	2.4
5.10	Ratio of net position in commodities to own funds	2.4	2.3	2.5	2.5

the aggregation process and to help in the identification of outliers, clustering of problems, or tiering in markets, there also were calls for more information on the distribution or dispersion of observations.

Several respondents identified the ratio of gross nonperforming loans to total loans as useful, in lieu of the FSI in the survey that used total assets as the denominator.

VIII Compilation and Dissemination Practices

The second part of the survey, the *Compilation and Dissemination Questionnaire*, requested information on the types of FSIs compiled, the availability of components that could be used to compile FSIs, and national practices in disseminating FSIs; the periodicity of compilation and dissemination; and various accounting, regulatory, and statistical practices related to FSIs.

Compilation and Dissemination of FSIs and Their Components

Country practices on the compilation and dissemination of FSIs and their components are mixed.[92] With only a few exceptions, compilation of FSIs themselves is quite limited, and dissemination of FSIs—especially outside the industrial countries—is scanty. However, compilation and dissemination of components of FSIs are more extensive.[93]

Table 8.1 provides information (by usefulness group) on the extent to which each FSI is compiled and disseminated. On *compilation*, the table shows that:

- Only 6 FSIs—all related to capital adequacy or the distribution of loans—are compiled by half or more of the respondents, with three FSIs each from Groups I and II indicators, respectively.

- Twenty-nine FSIs are compiled by one-quarter to one-half of the respondents.

- Twenty-one FSIs are compiled by less than one-quarter of all respondents.

On *dissemination*, the table shows that:

- Only two FSIs (Basel capital adequacy ratio and distribution of loans by sector) are disseminated

by half or more of the respondents; both of these FSIs are Group I indicators.

- Fourteen FSIs are disseminated by one-quarter to one-half of all respondents.

- Forty FSIs (75 percent of the total) are disseminated by less than one-quarter of all respondents.

In contrast, the compilation and dissemination of the *components used to construct FSIs* are much more extensive. For example, 81 percent of all respondents compile the components of the ratio of liquid assets to liquid liabilities, but only 40 percent of them compile the ratio itself. Table 8.1 also shows the extent to which the components of FSIs are compiled and disseminated.[94]

On compilation, Table 8.1 shows that while only 6 FSIs are compiled by *half or more of the respondents* (as noted above), the components of 30 FSIs are compiled by half or more of the respondents. Importantly, these 30 FSIs[95] for which components are extensively compiled comprise:

- All 13 of the Group I FSIs identified by users as most useful;

- Twelve or 44 percent of the Group II FSIs identified by users as useful; and

- Five or 36 percent of the Group III FSIs identified by users as moderately useful.

In addition, while the 6 FSIs noted above cover only 50 percent and 25 percent of the indicators in the capital adequacy and asset quality (lending) categories, respectively, the 30 FSIs span a much wider range of categories with sizeably higher shares, as follows: capital adequacy (67 percent of the indicators); asset quality (lending) (75 percent); profitability and competitiveness (100 percent); liquidity (45 percent); and sensitivity to market risk (30 percent).

---

[92]Appendix IV, Table A4.4 provides detailed information on the compilation and dissemination of FSIs.

[93]Components refer to the numerators or denominators that allow an indicator to be compiled or elements of the numerator or denominator that allow each, and hence the indicator itself, to be compiled.

[94]Table 4.3 reports figures for the least available component of each FSI because all components must be available in order to compile the FSI.

[95]A summary presentation of the 30 FSIs is shown in Appendix IV, Table A4.1.

Table 8.1. FSIs: Compilation and Dissemination Practices

FSI		Usefulness Score	Percent Compiling FSIs	Percent Disseminating FSIs	Percent Compiling Components	Percent Disseminating Components
Group I FSIs (average usefulness ratings of 3.5 to 4.0)						
1.1	Basel Capital Adequacy Ratio	3.8	91	57	91	57
1.1a	Ratio of Basel tier I capital to risk-weighted assets	3.6	87	47	87	65
2.4	Distribution of loans, by sector	3.6	82	65	82	43
2.5	Distribution of credit extended, by sector	3.5	49	38	57	44
2.8	Ratio of total large loans to own funds	3.5	31	9	56	22
2.9	Ratio of gross nonperforming loans to total assets	3.9	45	30	86	55
2.10	Ratio of nonperforming loans net of provisions to total assets	3.8	42	24	75	45
3.2	Ratios of profits to period-average assets (ROA)	3.6	45	31	81	48
3.3	Ratios of profits to period-average equity (ROE)	3.6	47	33	80	49
3.4	Ratio of net interest income to total income	3.5	42	25	88	58
3.8	Spread between reference lending and deposit rates	3.5	27	17	57	49
4.3	Ratio of liquid assets to total assets	3.5	40	22	81	44
4.4	Ratio of liquid assets to liquid liabilities	3.6	40	24	77	42
Group II FSIs (average usefulness ratings of 3.0 to 3.4)						
1.1b	Ratio of Basel tier I + tier II capital to risk-weighted assets	3.4	85	46	85	46
1.1c	Ratio of Basel tier I + II + III capital to risk-weighted assets	3.0	39	23	39	23
1.2	Distribution of capital adequacy ratios (number of institutions within specified capital adequacy ratio ranges)	3.3	23	12	23	12
1.3	Ratio of total on-balance-sheet assets to own funds	3.2	37	18	83	58
2.1	Distribution of on-balance-sheet assets, by Basel risk-weight category	3.4	83	35	83	35
2.4a	Loans for investment in commercial real estate	3.2	44	32	44	32
2.4b	Loans for investment in residential real estate	3.2	55	43	55	43
2.6	Distribution of credit extended, by country or region	3.1	45	30	52	35
2.7	Ratio of credit to related entities to total credit	3.4	28	8	68	23
2.11	Ratio of corporate debt to own funds ("debt-equity ratio")	3.4	18	10	37	27
2.12	Ratio of corporate profits to equity	3.3	16	10	42	27
2.13	Ratio of corporate debt-service costs to total corporate income	3.2	14	10	33	20
2.14	Corporate net foreign currency exposure	3.2	6	2	19	10
2.15	Ratio of household total debt to GDP	3.0	14	8	27	17
3.5	Ratio of trading and foreign exchange gains/losses to total income	3.3	32	17	69	44
3.6	Ratio of operating costs to net interest income	3.4	41	23	87	57
3.7	Ratio of staff costs to operating costs	3.2	40	23	84	54
4.5	Average maturity of assets	3.4	19	5	34	18
4.6	Average maturity of liabilities	3.4	19	5	37	18
4.10	Ratio of customer deposits to total (noninterbank) loans	3.2	35	15	85	65
5.1	Ratio of gross foreign currency assets to own funds	3.1	26	10	54	44
5.2	Ratio of net foreign currency position to own funds	3.4	27	12	76	24
5.3	Average interest rate repricing period for assets	3.0	18	4	18	4
5.4	Average interest rate repricing period for liabilities	3.0	17	3	17	3
5.5	Duration of assets	3.2	24	10	24	10
5.6	Duration of liabilities	3.2	23	8	23	8
5.8	Ratio of net equity position to own funds	3.0	16	9	27	14
Group III FSIs (average usefulness ratings of 2.5 to 2.9)						
2.2	Ratio of total gross asset position in financial derivatives to own funds	2.8	16	5	33	12

Table 8.1 *(concluded)*

FSI	Usefulness Score	Percent Compiling FSIs	Percent Disseminating FSIs	Percent Compiling Components	Percent Disseminating Components
2.3 Ratio of total gross liability position in financial derivatives to own funds	2.8	14	5	31	12
2.15a Ratio of household mortgage debt to GDP	2.8	27	17	27	17
2.15b Ratio of household debt owed to depository corporations to GDP	2.9	31	25	31	25
2.16 Number of applications for protection from creditors	2.7	14	11	14	11
3.1 Rate of change in number of depository corporations	2.7	38	30	62	46
3.9 Share of assets of the three largest depository corporations in total assets of depository corporations	2.9	38	17	72	32
4.1 Distribution of three-month local currency interbank rates for different depository corporations	2.9	25	13	25	13
4.2 Average interbank bid-ask spread for three-month local currency deposits	2.9	19	12	19	12
4.7 Average daily turnover in the treasury bill (or central bank bill) market	2.8	35	26	35	26
4.8 Average bid-ask spread in the treasury bill (or central bank bill) market	2.8	27	15	27	15
4.9 Ratio of central bank credit to depository corporations to depository corporations' total liabilities	2.9	22	12	72	53
4.11 Ratio of customer foreign currency deposits to total (noninterbank) foreign currency loans	2.9	26	12	74	47
5.7 Ratio of gross equity position to own funds	2.9	23	9	59	34
Group IV FSIs (average usefulness ratings of 2.4 and under)					
5.9 Ratio of gross position in commodities to own funds	2.4	8	2	16	6
5.10 Ratio of net position in commodities to own funds	2.4	9	3	15	5

On dissemination, the result is the same as for compilation, albeit to a lesser degree. Table 8.1 shows that while only two FSIs (as noted above) are disseminated by half or more of the respondents, the components of 8 FSIs are disseminated by half or more of the respondents.[96]

The results on component compilation in particular suggest that many countries may be in a position to compile a good number of FSIs (especially the Group I FSIs), although significant gaps remain.[97]

Box 8.1 discusses how compilation and dissemination practices differ by type of economy.

In general, the broad availability of many components of FSIs derives from the accounting, statistical, tax, and registration systems that can be tapped for generating data on the components of FSIs, among which monetary statistics[98] and supervisory reports on banks' balance sheets and income are among the most important.

Finally, since one of the objectives of the survey was to evaluate whether the Special Data Dissemination Standard (SDDS) or other vehicles would be appropriate to encourage dissemination of FSIs, it was encouraging that the response rate of SDDS sub-

---

[96]Several countries indicate that some FSIs are disseminated while their components are not. If these FSIs are included with the pool of FSIs whose components are disseminated, there would be 13 FSIs altogether (instead of the 8 indicated above) that are potentially available for dissemination.

[97]For example, the results suggest that systems to compile statistics on financial derivatives and the financial condition of nonfinancial sectors are not widely available, as indicated by the limited degree to which components are compiled for FSIs number 2.2—Ratio of total asset position in derivatives to total own funds, 2.3—Ratio of total liability position in derivatives to total own funds, 2.13—Ratio of corporate debt service to income, 2.14—Corporate net foreign currency exposure, and 2.15—Ratio of household debt to GDP.

---

[98]Monetary statistics published in the IMF's *International Financial Statistics* are the most comprehensive source for internationally comparable aggregate data on countries' financial systems. Monetary statistics are compiled on a high-frequency monthly basis within an existing institutional framework, and internationally agreed compilation standards exist, as embodied in the IMF's *Monetary and Financial Statistics Manual*. Similarly, euro area monetary statistics are used as a key element of the European Central Bank's program on macroprudential indicators.

Box 8.1. Compilation and Dissemination Practices by Type of Economy

The average number of FSIs compiled and disseminated by industrial, emerging, and developing countries are shown in the first figure.[1] Industrial countries compile and disseminate the largest number of FSIs and emerging countries compile and disseminate the second largest number of FSIs. Industrial and emerging countries compile on average more than half of the indicators specified in the survey.

Average Number of FSIs Compiled and Desseminated by Type of Economy[1]

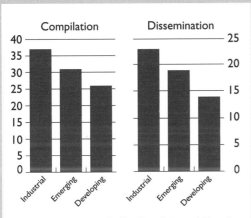

Source: IMF Survey on the Use, Compilation, and Dissemination of Macroprudential Indicators.

[1]Figures in parentheses indicate the number of indicators compiled as a percentage of the total number of indicators included in the survey.

A comparison of the number of FSIs compiled and disseminated indicates that around 60 percent of compiled FSIs are disseminated; this percentage is broadly the same for each type of economy. Divergence be-

tween the number of FSIs compiled and disseminated indicates that the private sector has access to a narrower range of financial soundness indicators than is available to national authorities. It also indicates that there is scope for increasing the number of publicly available indicators of financial sector soundness in all types of economies.

The second figure reports on the percentage of indicators compiled in each FSI category disaggregated by type of economy. It shows that industrial countries in general compile the highest percentage of indicators in each category of FSI, followed by emerging and developing countries. The one exception is in the category of *liquidity*, where emerging countries compile the highest percentage of indicators. Notably, industrial countries compile a significantly larger percentage of indicators on *asset quality (borrowing institution)* than emerging and developing countries, probably reflecting the greater amount of statistical resources needed to compile indicators in that category.

Percentage of Indicators Compiled in each Category by Type of Economy

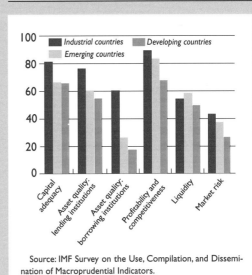

Source: IMF Survey on the Use, Compilation, and Dissemination of Macroprudential Indicators.

[1]An FSI is counted as compiled and disseminated if the FSI itself, or all the components of the FSI, are compiled and disseminated.

scribers was very high—all but two of the 50 SDDS subscribers (as of December 2001) had completed the questionnaire.

For almost all FSIs, users in countries subscribing to the SDDS rated the usefulness of FSIs nearly identically with users in industrial and emerging

countries, which indicated that their priorities are similar to those already discussed in the paper. Although subscribers' performance in the dissemination of components of FSIs is somewhat better, the overall results are broadly similar to those for the total population of respondents—that is, compilation

Table 8.2. Periodicity of FSIs

Practice	Users' Preference	Compilation Practice	Dissemination
Capital adequacy	Quarterly/monthly	Quarterly/monthly	Quarterly/monthly
Asset quality (lending institution)	Quarterly/monthly	Monthly/quarterly	Monthly/quarterly
Asset quality (borrowing institution)	Quarterly/other/annual	Annual/quarterly	Annual
Profitability and competitiveness	Quarterly	Quarterly	Annual/quarterly
Liquidity	Monthly	Monthly	Monthly
Sensitivity to market risks	Quarterly/monthly/other	Monthly	N/A*

*Too few responses were received to produce valid results.

and dissemination of FSIs by subscribers is limited but compilation and dissemination of components is more extensive. Appendix IV, Table A4.2 provides information on the compilation and dissemination of FSIs and their components by SDDS subscribers.

Periodicity

The survey also inquired about country practices regarding the periodicity of compilation and dissemination, as well as users' needs in those areas. On the latter, users were asked to indicate whether the periodicity for FSIs should be monthly, quarterly, semi-annually, annually, or other specified periodicity (such as daily or weekly).

Table 8.2 lists, for each category of FSI, the existing compilation and dissemination practices and the most common periodicity sought by users. Each cell lists the most common periodicity (compiled or sought) and any other periodicity compiled or sought at least 80 percent as often as the most common.

As shown in the first column of Table 8.2, users clearly seek quarterly or monthly data for all the major categories of FSIs. Although quarterly data are sought most often in five of the six categories, monthly data are sought almost as often. For liquidity FSIs, a number of respondents sought higher frequency data, such as daily or weekly.

In terms of compilation, FSIs are compiled monthly in about 42 percent of all cases,[99] and quarterly in about 34 percent of all cases. The FSIs compiled on a monthly basis are mainly capital adequacy indicators from banking supervision data, asset quality (lending institution) indicators derived from monthly monetary

statistics or monetary statistics' source data, and some liquidity and sensitivity to market risks indicators derived from high-frequency source data. Quarterly series predominate in the profitability category and are nearly as common as monthly series in the categories for capital adequacy and asset quality (lending institutions). Data are compiled annually most often within the category of asset quality (borrowing institutions). "Other" periodicities most often refer to daily or weekly compilations of FSIs related to interest rates or securities market turnover.

The periodicity of dissemination of FSIs vary considerably between the different categories of FSIs. No general pattern could be ascertained and the number of responses was too low for valid conclusions to be made.

Accounting, Regulatory, and Statistical Issues

Information relating to accounting and regulatory issues and statistical standards was sought in order to gain insights into whether international best practices exist and into the international comparability of FSIs. The information was drawn from Part IIb of the *Compilation and Dissemination Questionnaire*.

International Comparability of FSIs

The *Compilation and Dissemination Questionnaire* asked a series of quantitative and open-ended questions about accounting and statistical issues in order to assess the state of existing practices; possibly identify best practices that might be used as a basis for development of international standards; and help identify strategies for improving the comparability of FSIs.

---

[99]A case refers to a single observation of an FSI by a respondent.

Box 8.2. Country Practices on Nonperforming Loans

Nonperforming loans (NPLs) carried by banks on their balance sheets and the provisions held by banks for loan losses are components of two of the most important FSIs identified in the survey: the ratios of gross NPLs to total assets and of NPLs net of provisions to capital. Both FSIs had high average usefulness scores and are compiled by more than 40 percent of the 93 respondents. The reason for their importance is that high levels of NPLs and inadequate provisioning can severely affect the profitability and eventually the solvency of the banking system. However, the survey results also suggest that there is as yet no international consensus on sound practices for recognizing NPLs and on appropriate levels of loan loss provisioning. This lack of consensus severely limits the international comparability of FSIs and impairs the ability of market analysts and regulators to monitor the financial system, particularly at the regional and global level.

The survey posed three supplementary open-ended questions on NPLs—regarding the respondent's system for recognizing NPLs; the rules governing the valuation of provisions; and the rules on accrual of interest on NPLs. The results suggest that practices differ considerably on the first two issues, although there is greater convergence on the third one.

Of the 28 respondents that provided a sufficient amount of information, there are generally three different methods by which substandard loans are recognized. Four respondents leave the matter of recognition to the discretion of banks—there is no specific system and banks have the responsibility to exercise their best judgment, which will then be assessed by external auditors and supervisors on a periodic basis. Eight respondents employ qualitative criteria, based upon well-defined weaknesses related to deterioration in the borrower's financial condition, inability of the borrower to generate cash flow to service debt in an orderly manner, and deterioration in secondary sources of repayment such as guarantor support and loss in the value of collateral. Sixteen respondents employ quantitative criteria, reflecting mainly the minimum period of delinquency in payments before recognition. However, this minimum period varies among the 16 respondents. Eleven respondents adopt a minimum delinquency period of 90 days, the most prevalent criterion. Three respondents adopt a tighter standard of 30 days; one respondent adopts a looser standard of 180 days; and one does not specify a minimum period but adopts the criterion of a "past due" exceeding 20 percent of exposure to the borrower as constituting a nonperforming loan.

On loan provisioning, 5 of the 24 respondents reporting a sufficient amount of information leave the extent of provisioning to the institution's discretion or best judgment. Four impose a qualitative criterion related to the estimated realizable value of the loan, such as the face value of the loan less the market value of collateral or the potential amount that can reasonably be deemed collectible. Fifteen respondents impose specific minimum standards, with an increasing level of provision depending on the degree of impairment of the loan. However, these minimum standards again differ across respondents. For the three respondents using 30 days of payment delinquency to recognize impairment, one specifies 20 percent, another 25 percent, and the third 30 percent as minimum required provisions. For the five respondents using 90 days as the criterion for impairment, one imposes 15 percent, two 20 percent, and two 25 percent as minimum required provisions. The respondent using 180 days as the impairment criterion specifies a 20 percent minimum provision. For the six respondents using qualitative criteria, three impose 20 percent, two impose 25 percent, and one imposes 30 percent as minimum required provisions.

There is greater convergence on the recognition of accrued interest for impaired loans. Of the 20 respondents providing a sufficient amount of information, 15 require the cessation of interest accrual on NPLs. Two allow recognition of accrued interest for substandard loans but require provisions for the amount accrued. Two allow accrued interest to be recorded in suspense accounts. One allows interest to be accrued and reflected in the profit and loss account until it becomes very probable that the interest will not be paid.

The Basel Committee on Banking Supervision has taken up the task of setting standards for recognition of substandard loans and for determining loan loss provisioning. The Committee has called for the timely recognition and measurement of impaired loans to be made in accordance with documented policies and on the basis of fundamental accounting concepts, and for adequacy of provisions to absorb the estimated losses associated with the loan portfolio. The Committee has also recommended that interest accrual should cease when a loan becomes impaired or, if the accrual is continued, that a provision for the full amount of the accrual be made.

The responses highlighted a diversity of national practices and revealed many reasons why FSIs might not be comparable across economies:

- Different, and often complex, standards exist for recognizing substandard claims and provisioning (see Box 8.2);

- National definitions of regulatory capital differ—for instance, as regards deductions and components of each tier of capital. Moreover, numerous countries indicated that they have not approved the use of tier III capital within the base;

- Consolidation practices for foreign branches and subsidiaries differ (see section below). Within each country, some FSIs use global consolidations drawn from supervisory data, while other FSIs use national consolidations drawn from statistical sources. Overall, however, some international conformity in consolidation exists because of the rather widespread use of national consolidations;

- Valuation practices for financial instruments differ (see section below). Key issues include the limited use of market valuations for debt securities and shares, and diverse practices for on-balance-sheet recognition of derivatives, repurchase agreements, and securities lending;

- Different rules exist for revaluing foreign currency positions. Although there appears to be convergence in industrial countries toward use of market exchange rates in revaluing foreign currency-denominated positions, continued use of official rates in a number of emerging and developing countries might hinder the comparability of FSIs.

The list of issues above indicates that practices are diverse and that cross-country comparison of FSIs is challenging. International harmonization of FSIs would be a significant undertaking.

In January 2000, the Executive Board of the IMF decided that a two-pronged strategy for promoting the international comparability of FSIs would be pursued, in which initial work would use existing, unharmonized data, but over time efforts would be made to foster greater harmonization of FSIs. To allow users to evaluate data, descriptions (metadata) of the accounting and statistical standards and practices used should accompany dissemination of FSIs.

Consolidation

The survey sought information on country practices for consolidating information on foreign branches and subsidiaries of financial institutions into single accounting statements or statistical reports. A key issue is whether data are compiled using a national or global consolidation. A national consolidation focuses on bank operations within the national boundaries, which is the main policy focus of national authorities, whereas a global consolidation captures information on the global risks and financial strengths and exposures of the worldwide enterprise. Different areas of analysis might require different types of consolidation.

The survey found strong differences in practices by type of economy. Respondents in developing countries adhered overwhelmingly to a national resi-

dency consolidation basis for most FSIs. This possibly reflects that banks headquartered in many developing countries have few or no nonresident branches or subsidiaries. It might also reflect limited supervisory infrastructures that could not effectively monitor and supervise nonresident operations. To some extent, respondents in emerging countries also reported this adherence to the use of national consolidations. In industrial countries, supervisors used global consolidations most often, but also reported that both global and national consolidation data were available for numerous FSIs.[100]

The survey also found differences in practices by category of FSI. These differences often reflect whether the primary source data are supervisory or statistical in nature. A summary of the practices by category of FSI is shown below.

- *Capital adequacy.* In industrial and emerging countries, data are primarily from supervisory sources and are generally on a global consolidation basis, although both global and national consolidations are often available. A number of emerging economies and many developing economies only use national consolidations. In terms of worldwide totals, both consolidations are available about equally, and for some FSIs up to one-quarter of respondents use both consolidations. A small number of countries report nonstandard consolidations in their data, such as including nonresident branches but excluding nonresident subsidiaries.

- *Asset quality (lending institutions).* FSIs derived from monetary statistics are overwhelmingly on a national consolidation basis; FSIs derived from supervisory sources are most often on a global consolidation basis, but in many cases are on a national basis or are available on both bases.

- *Asset quality (borrowing institutions).* FSIs are almost exclusively on a national consolidation basis because the underlying data are drawn from national macroeconomic statistical series.

- *Profitability and competitiveness.* Data are most often on a national consolidation basis or are available on both bases. However, a number of countries have data only on a global basis. Within the profitability category, nonstandard consolidations are used by a number of countries.

---

[100]The availability of FSI data on both consolidation bases could have some important advantages. For example, one respondent noted, "The survey does not address the main statistical aspect, which is reconciliation between the home and host country approach, which will be viable if both supervisory and macroeconomic statistical data sources are used."

Table 8.3. Valuation Practices Affecting FSIs by Data Source
(All countries; number of responses)

	General Valuation Method Used						Valuation Method for Foreign Currency Denominated Instruments					
	Method[1]				Frequency of revaluations[2]		Conversion exchange rate[3]				Frequency of revaluations[4]	
	H	M	L	O	B	O	E	A	G	O	B	O
1. Supervisory data sources												
a. Deposits	62	6	1	5	47	9	39	5	24	2	61	5
b. Loans	56	5	4	8	45	9	40	5	22	2	59	6
c. Securities (other than shares)	20	23	11	17	51	14	39	5	20	3	50	12
d. Shares and other equity	19	24	12	15	54	12	37	4	22	4	51	12
e. Financial derivatives	9	30	1	13	37	14	33	4	14	3	36	13
f. Miscellaneous receivables/payables	52	7	4	6	43	11	37	5	21	3	56	7
g. Nonfinancial assets	41	9	8	13	42	15	32	4	21	6	49	8
2. Statistical data sources												
a. Deposits	42	4	0	1	29	6	27	2	17	2	36	9
b. Loans	40	3	0	4	27	7	27	2	15	2	33	10
c. Securities (other than shares)	14	19	7	7	31	10	29	2	13	2	34	10
d. Shares and other equity	14	20	6	5	30	9	27	2	13	2	32	10
e. Financial derivatives	8	18	2	5	20	11	22	2	9	3	23	11
f. Miscellaneous receivables/payables	35	3	3	1	24	7	25	2	13	2	32	8
g. Nonfinancial assets	22	8	3	10	28	8	24	2	12	2	32	7
3. Other data sources												
a. Deposits	9	2	0	1	8	0	7	0	4	1	10	1
b. Loans	10	1	0	2	8	1	7	0	3	1	9	1
c. Securities (other than shares)	3	6	1	1	8	2	7	0	4	1	9	2
d. Shares and other equity	4	6	0	1	8	2	7	0	4	1	9	2
e. Financial derivatives	1	5	0	1	5	2	6	0	2	1	6	2
f. Miscellaneous receivables/payables	9	1	0	1	8	0	6	0	3	1	8	1
g. Nonfinancial assets	5	3	1	2	7	1	6	0	3	0	7	1

[1]H = Historic cost; M = Market price/fair value; L = Lower of cost or market; O = Other.

[2]B = On-balance-sheet date; O = Other.

[3]E = Market rate (end period); A = Market rate (period average); G = Official rate; O = Other.

[4]B = On-balance-sheet date; O = Other.

- *Liquidity*. National consolidations are most common, but the FSIs on liquid assets and average maturities of assets and liabilities are often on a global basis. Global consolidation is not relevant for some of the liquidity FSIs that refer solely to national conditions.

- *Sensitivity to market risks*. National consolidations are most common. Global consolidations are used to some extent in supervisory data in industrial and emerging countries.

Valuation

The survey requested information on national practices in valuing financial instruments, with separate information requested for foreign currency denominated-instruments. Respondents indicated, for each major type of instrument, the type of valuation method used—historical cost, market value, the lower of cost or market, or other. The survey requested separate information for each major source of data—supervisory, statistical, and other. Table 8.3 summarizes the results.

Broadly similar patterns exist for all three types of source data. For deposits and loans, respondents most commonly use historical valuations—in at least three-quarters of all responses in supervisory data and in about nine out of ten cases in statistical data.[101] In contrast, for securities (other than shares) and shares and other equity, no valuation method clearly predominates, although respondents use mar-

---

[101]Use of historical valuations is in accordance with international statistical standards.

ket values more often than the other valuation approaches. For example, market values for shares and other equity are used in 40 percent of all cases, historical valuations in 29 percent of cases, and the lower of cost or market and other valuations in 14 and 17 percent of cases, respectively. For financial derivatives, respondents use market valuations most often, with supervisors also reporting fairly common use of "other" valuations, which they sometimes indicated were hedge valuations. Historical valuations predominate in miscellaneous receivables and payables and in nonfinancial assets, but use of the other three types of valuations is not uncommon.

On the translation of the value of foreign currency-denominated instruments into domestic currency equivalents, respondents use end-of-period exchange rates most often for all types of financial instruments. A large minority of emerging and developing countries reported that they used official exchange rates. Foreign currency positions were revalued most often at the rate applying on the balance sheet closing date. However, revaluations of foreign currency positions at other frequencies were not uncommon for securities (other than shares), shares and other equities, and financial derivatives.

IX Analytical Frameworks and Research

This chapter discusses the responses to the supplementary questions included in the *User Questionnaire* to gather information on methods of macroprudential analysis, the institutional coverage of such analyses, preferences on the statistical presentation of FSIs, and the use of business surveys to complement macroprudential analysis.

Macroprudential Research

The majority of the survey respondents (76 percent) reported doing macroprudential research or analysis.[102] Most respondents said they analyzed conditions in the banking sector, both at the aggregate level and at the level of the individual bank—although some analysts (mostly supervisors) also analyzed conditions in subsets of banks, classified by different categories and peer groups. Although the analysis typically focused on the private banking sector, several countries also reported separately monitoring and analyzing developments in specific depository institutions' subsectors (e.g., state-owned banks and cooperatives), in the nondepository institutions' sector and subsectors, and in financial markets.

Most of the analysis was based on individual bank prudential data (consistent with the higher response rate among supervisors) derived from both on-site and off-site inspections. However, the prudential data were often supplemented with macroeconomic and market information (especially the evolution of asset prices) and, in a few cases, with data on the condition of debtors.

Most respondents mentioned using CAMELS-type frameworks to analyze institutions but many also used statistical models, particularly early warning models and models based on descriptive statistics such as correlations and trends in key indicators (e.g., credit growth and asset quality). In addition,

some respondents used time series models while several others used qualitative analysis and stress tests, and a few used analytical frameworks such as the financial accelerator model.[103] The primary objective of the analysis was the assessment of risks, covering equally credit, interest rate, foreign exchange, liquidity, and macroeconomic risks.

The analysis was sometimes published as part of an agency's annual report or as a stand-alone document—particularly when it was performed on the financial system as a whole or on a particular sector within the system. However, the information was usually used solely for internal evaluations.

Coverage of Financial Institutions

Importance of Nondepository Financial Institutions

About 80 percent of the respondents reported that information on nondepository financial institutions, markets, and activities was important to the overall analysis of financial sector soundness. On nondepository financial institutions,[104] the majority of the respondents were most interested in information on insurance corporations and pension funds, followed by other financial intermediaries (Figure 9.1). Respondents viewed many of these institutions as playing an important role in financial intermediation and possibly in contagion. Several respondents mentioned the importance of specialized financial intermediaries such as venture capital funds for advanced economies; and microcredit institutions and development banks or funds for developing countries.

---

[102]Of those who reported doing some sort of research, 61 percent were supervisors, 25 percent were policy or research analysts, and 14 percent were market or other participants. These percentages are similar to the relative weight of each group in the response sample.

[103]Financial accelerator models are based on information asymmetries between borrowers and lenders. They postulate that when economic conditions are depressed and corporate net worth is low, access to credit is reduced even for worthwhile borrowers. When conditions improve and corporate net worth increases, renewed access to credit by borrowers adds to the economic stimulus. In both cases, the effects are procyclical. See also Chapter IV.

[104]Defined as insurance corporations and pension funds, other financial intermediaries, and financial auxiliaries in line with the IMF's *Monetary and Financial Statistics Manual*.

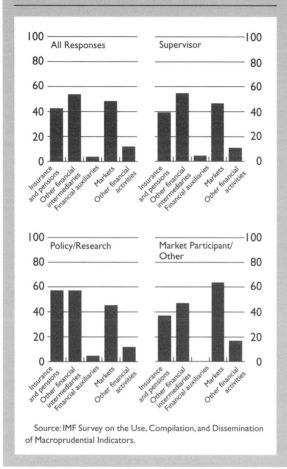

Figure 9.1. Institutional Coverage of Analysis
(As a percentage of total responses per category)

Source: IMF Survey on the Use, Compilation, and Dissemination of Macroprudential Indicators.

rations while a few others mentioned the importance of monitoring other financial activity, such as the functioning of payment, settlement, and clearing systems. In addition, some respondents emphasized that qualitative information—such as the thoroughness of supervision and the transparency of financial policies—was important to the overall assessment of financial sector stability.

Disaggregation of "Depository Corporations" into Subsectors

Almost 60 percent of the respondents thought that more disaggregated information on depository corporations was needed, particularly breakdowns by ownership, function, exposure to risk (e.g., geographical, asset type, borrower type, etc.) and size (Figure 9.2). A few respondents felt that disaggregated data that highlighted distributions among

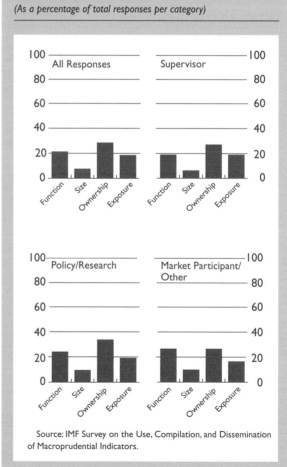

Figure 9.2. Factors Used to Identify Key Subsectors
(As a percentage of total responses per category)

Source: IMF Survey on the Use, Compilation, and Dissemination of Macroprudential Indicators.

Some respondents noted the importance of information on financial conglomerates, especially those that included insurance companies.

On financial markets, about 90 percent of those responding on the issue indicated that data on the securities markets (public and private debt and equity markets) were important.[105] A few thought that information on foreign exchange markets (16 percent) and derivatives markets (6 percent) was also important.

Several respondents noted that borrower information (indebtedness and asset-liability mismatches) was useful as it provided some indication on emerging credit quality trends and risks in the corporate, household, or foreign sectors. Some respondents said that they paid particular attention to large corpo-

---

[105]The types of data mentioned included trading volumes, bid-ask spreads, and credit spreads.

banks or allowed for peer group analysis was also useful; one respondent felt that the breakdown of banks should be as fine as possible to enable isolation of distinctive activity patterns. Several stressed that the type of disaggregation would depend on the issue being analyzed, however.

Almost 30 percent of all respondents (about half of those who felt that more disaggregation was useful) mentioned that they analyzed or would like to analyze institutions by ownership characteristics (e.g., domestic versus foreign, private versus state-owned, and publicly held stock versus privately held equity). Of these respondents, almost all stated that a breakdown between domestic and foreign institutions was useful, with some saying that the domestic/foreign distinction was important because foreign institutions might operate under different regulatory and supervisory regimes. At the same time, a quarter of the respondents stated that a breakdown between private and state-owned institutions was important.

About 20 percent of the respondents said that disaggregation by function or exposure was useful. The functions most often mentioned were commercial banking, universal banking, and specialized banking (especially mortgage lending and, to a lesser extent, development lending). About 80 percent of the respondents interested in disaggregation by exposure indicated that they would like information on internationally active banks. Sixteen percent wanted disaggregated information on offshore banks, while another 16 percent wanted information on banks disaggregated by their geographical market.

Only about 7 percent of respondents mentioned that disaggregating the sector by size or separating out systemically important institutions was useful. However, respondents may have underemphasized this factor since it was the subject of a separate question.

Systemically Important Institutions

Almost 60 percent of the respondents reported doing some evaluation of systemically important institutions. Supervisors tended to be more concerned about such institutions—two-thirds of them reported that they evaluated the condition of these institutions, as opposed to less than half of market participants and about half of the government policy or research analysts.

Most respondents reported using a measure of size (of assets and/or deposits) to ascertain the importance of an institution. Sometimes size was coupled with other criteria—for instance, exposure to certain risks (such as foreign exchange risk), complexity of transactions, or complexity of ownership structure. However, some respondents only mentioned risk exposure, or used legal or prudential definitions, while others evaluated all institutions by sector or a partic-

ular category—which indicated that all institutions within a particular classification (e.g., problem banks, deposit-taking institutions, institutions with insured deposits, commercial banks, and international banks) were sometimes considered systemically important. This was often the case in countries with small, developing, or concentrated markets.

Many respondents said that the techniques used to evaluate the condition of systemically important institutions were similar to those used to evaluate other institutions. Most mentioned using the CAMELS framework or ratio analysis, while some used early warning models, other statistical models (e.g., Value at Risk), and market assessments (e.g., ratings) to inform their evaluations. Many respondents also used techniques such as increased supervision, including increased on-site examinations, reports from management, meetings with management, and external audits. Among the variables stressed by the respondents as important in their evaluations were interbank activity, liquidity, large exposures, foreign exchange exposure, consolidated positions for institutions that are part of a financial group, and risk management practices (including assessing internal models).

Of the respondents that evaluated systemically important institutions, a slight majority said that the institutions were not subject to enhanced statistical or disclosure requirements, although some stressed that they were nonetheless subject to more intense supervision. Of the respondents that mentioned enhanced statistical or disclosure requirements, most required more frequent, extensive, or detailed reporting, as well as more frequent on-site examinations. Many respondents did not address this part of the question, however, making the results difficult to interpret.

Norms, Benchmarks, and Thresholds

Many respondents reported that specific norms, benchmarks, or thresholds were not used in macroprudential analysis. While some of them were considering using norms and benchmarks in the future, others preferred using comparisons with peer group countries to establish relative rankings.

Among those who reported using norms and benchmarks for FSIs, some highlighted their critical role in guiding interpretation of the indicators. For this purpose, benchmarks were constructed in a number of ways, including (1) historical averages, (2) bank supervisors' prudential thresholds applied at the aggregate level, (3) trigger points, (4) cross-country comparisons, and (5) criteria constructed from econometric studies.

Many respondents mentioned that benchmarks were widely used in the implementation of prudential standards, however. Since the majority of respondents had implemented the recommendations from the Basel Committee on Banking Supervision, the Basel recommendations in an aggregate form were commonly used as benchmarks. Some respondents also mentioned international best practice as the basis for forming their benchmarks. Overall, many respondents had adopted benchmarks or thresholds for capital adequacy ratios, liquidity, foreign exchange exposures, and reserve requirements. However, warning level thresholds were applied primarily to individual banking institutions rather than to the system as a whole.

Presentation

Generally, the majority of respondents preferred the use of ratios and growth rates in presenting their FSIs. However, many respondents also felt that the preferred mode of presentation depended on the particular FSI in question and the type of analysis being conducted. For example, for sectoral aggregates, it was useful to have weighted averages as well as simple averages, accompanied by the frequency distribution of institutions according to range of values of the indicators.

In this connection, some respondents noted that measures of dispersion (standard deviations, histograms, Gini indices, etc.) could be particularly useful in presenting FSIs because they allowed the analyst to identify outliers, trends in concentration, or tiering in markets, etc., which could be relevant for the analysis of financial stability.

Figure 9.3 contains a breakdown of responses by mode of presentation and by type of user. The category "depends on FSI" is not exclusive—that is, some respondents identified several preferred modes of presentation but nonetheless indicated that it depended on the FSI or the type of analysis. The N/A column presents the percentage of responses that were either not applicable or not completed.

Composite Measures[106]

Overall, the proportion of respondents that reported using composite measures (36 percent) was only slightly less than the proportion that did not use

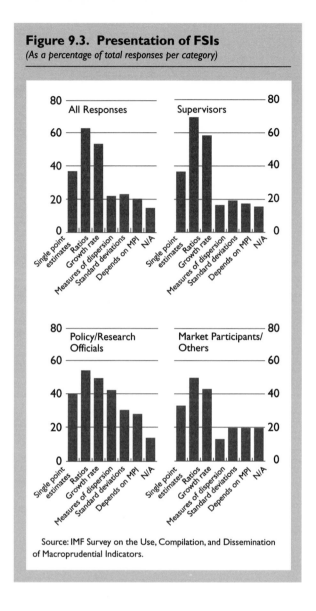

Figure 9.3. Presentation of FSIs
(As a percentage of total responses per category)

Source: IMF Survey on the Use, Compilation, and Dissemination of Macroprudential Indicators.

them (38 percent). However, this result obscures the fact that there was substantial variation across user types. For example, while 41 percent of supervisors reported using composite measures, only 29 percent of respondents engaged in policy/research and 23 percent of market participants/others said that they used such measures. Furthermore, 25 percent of all respondents either said that they were not familiar with the concept or the question was not applicable, or simply did not respond. A few mentioned that they were considering the use of such measures in the future, however. One respondent, for instance, replied that there were plans to establish composite measures of the condition of the financial system, although none of the prototypes had yet been adopted due to their instability.

---

[106]The possibility of developing a composite indicator of financial system soundness was discussed at the 1999 Consultative Meeting on macroprudential indicators. There was a general sense that the complex reality of financial markets may not lend itself to being captured in such indicators. In particular, composite indicators could prove simplistic and potentially misleading, as they may conceal or misrepresent problems by offsetting positive and negative signals from different individual components.

Among the respondents using composite measures, most used single point estimates, ratios, and growth rates to construct them. Many stated that composite measures were based on the compiled data from balance sheets, income statements, and other statistical reports. Some countries also reported using early warning system-type models—which mostly used macroeconomic variables and not FSIs—to produce a composite measure. These models would make these measures leading indicators of a potential financial crisis, instead of concurrent indicators of the condition of the financial system.

Business Surveys

Overall, about half of all respondents reported that they made use of business survey results—qualitative or quantitative measures of business expectations and potential leading indicators of instability—to supplement macroprudential analysis. The group making the most use of business surveys (with 56 percent) was policy/research officials involved in the analysis of financial system soundness. About half of all supervisors and market participants/others mentioned that they used business surveys.

X Concluding Remarks

Identification of Core and Encouraged Sets of FSIs

Empirical and analytical evidence on the usefulness of specific FSIs as well as the results of the survey on macroprudential indicators were used to identify core and encouraged sets of FSIs. The IMF Executive Board discussed these FSI sets at a meeting in June 2001.[107]

To identify these sets, six criteria were applied:

- focus on core markets and institutions;
- analytical significance;
- revealed usefulness;
- relevance in most circumstances (i.e., not country-specific);
- availability; and
- parsimony (achieving the maximum information content with a limited number of FSIs).

Ideally, indicators included in the core set should also be comparable across countries—which would be possible if countries adhere to internationally agreed prudential, accounting, and statistical standards—to facilitate monitoring of the financial system, not only at the national but also at the global level. The latter is important in view of the magnitude and mobility of international capital, and the risk of contagion of financial crises from one country to another. Advancing international comparability of FSIs and convergence toward best practice are important goals for further work in this area. In the near term, most of these FSIs can be compiled from unharmonized national data that reflect different supervisory and accounting practices. Over the longer term, if FSIs are to be comparable across countries, it will be important to address harmonization of underlying accounting standards, aggregation and consolidation issues, and asset valuation, classification, and provisioning rules. The usefulness of the core set of FSIs can be enhanced if national authorities provide, along with the FSIs, descriptions of the concepts and compilation practices used in their construction (i.e., the metadata). Metadata are particularly important in the absence of harmonization and resolution of the issues mentioned above.

Based on the criteria listed above, two key sets of FSIs were identified:[108]

- The *core set of 15 indicators*, listed in Table 10.1, is focused on the banking sector, and is considered to fulfill the six selection criteria mentioned above. (1) All indicators included in the core set focus on core institutions—the banking sector. (2) The analytical relevance of the five aspects of bank vulnerability covered by the core set, as well as of individual FSIs, is well documented in Chapter III of this paper.[109] (3) All indicators with usefulness ratings above 3.5—as identified in the survey—are included in this set.[110] (4) The FSIs in the core set are meaningful in most country circumstances—a conclusion that is supported by both analytical evidence and the results of the survey. (5) Compilation appears broadly feasible, given the relatively large number of countries that now compile these indicators or their components.[111] (6) It provides data covering all main categories of bank risk, within a limited set of indicators. The core set should have priority in future work on FSIs.

---

[107]A summary of the Board discussion can be found at http://www.imf.org/external/np/mae/fsi/2001/eng/062501.htm.

[108]An explanation of terms used to define the indicators can be found in Appendix I.

[109]Durations of assets and liabilities are examples of indicators that are highly relevant analytically—which is why they are included in the core set—although their compilation is not widespread. Appendix I offers alternative indicators in cases where durations are not easily available, at least in the short term.

[110]Two FSIs with usefulness ratings above 3.5 were not included on parsimony grounds as they capture aspects of bank vulnerability already covered by other FSIs. Some FSI definitions vary slightly from the ones used in the FSI Survey and they should be considered preliminary pending further work on the definition of FSIs.

[111]However, many countries would have to adjust existing data compilation programs to compile the core FSIs.

Table 10.1. Core Set of FSIs

Capital adequacy	Regulatory capital to risk-weighted assets
	Regulatory tier I capital to risk-weighted assets
Asset quality	Nonperforming loans to total gross loans
	Nonperforming loans net of provisions to capital
	Sectoral distribution of loans to total loans
	Large exposures to capital
Earnings and profitability	Return on assets (net income to average total assets)
	Return on equity (net income to average equity)
	Interest margin to gross income
	Noninterest expenses to gross income
Liquidity	Liquid assets to total assets (liquid asset ratio)
	Liquid assets to short-term liabilities
Sensitivity to market risk	Duration of assets
	Duration of liabilities
	Net open position in foreign exchange to capital

- The *encouraged set of 26 indicators,* listed in Table 10.2, includes additional indicators for deposit-taking institutions as well as data on other institutions and markets that are relevant in assessing financial stability. FSIs in this set are considered to fulfill some, but not all, of the selection criteria. FSIs on deposit-taking institutions included in the encouraged set may be particularly important in certain countries, but less so in others. In the case of nonbank financial intermediaries, further work is needed to obtain meaningful indicators of their health and soundness; the FSIs included in the set simply aim at capturing the importance of this sector in the financial system. Although FSIs for the corporate sector and real estate markets emerge from both analytical studies and the survey as critical to assessments of financial vulnerabilities, their compilation—in terms of number of countries and coverage—remains very limited. As a result of these limitations, the encouraged set is somewhat more tentative.

Working with two sets of FSIs—a core set and an encouraged set—avoids a one-size-fits-all approach, and provides a degree of flexibility in the selection of indicators that are most relevant to assessing vulnerabilities in country-specific circumstances. Indicators of the core set can be combined with selected, additional indicators of the encouraged set that might be of particular relevance in the country concerned, depending on its level of financial development, institutional structure, and regional circumstances.

Notably, within the encouraged set, indicators of the corporate sector and real estate markets may be considered as a priority in light of their analytical significance for assessing financial vulnerabilities in a wide variety of circumstances, and their compilation should be encouraged. The exact methodology of compilation, and the number and coverage of corporate indicators, will need to take into account the specific circumstances of countries. As soon as sufficient progress has been made in these areas, some of these indicators should be included in the core set.

Directions for Further Work

This paper has discussed the quantitative and, to some extent, qualitative elements of the macroprudential analysis of financial systems. This is ongoing work—at the IMF and elsewhere—and it is encouraging to see the growing interest in this subject among central banks and other national and international official institutions around the world.

The review highlights that work on measuring and analyzing FSIs has advanced substantially in recent years. At the same time, it points to specific areas where more work is needed.

- Definitional guidelines are necessary to arrive at clear definitions of the indicators, thereby advancing international comparability and convergence toward best practice. Looking ahead, the IMF is working to produce a *Compilation Guide on Financial Soundness Indicators* in order to facilitate, and encourage, national compilation of

---

Table 10.2. Encouraged Set of FSIs

Deposit-taking institutions	Capital to assets
	Geographical distribution of loans to total loans
	Gross asset position in financial derivatives to capital
	Gross liability position in financial derivatives to capital
	Trading income to total income
	Personnel expenses to noninterest expenses
	Spread between reference lending and deposit rates
	Spread between highest and lowest interbank rate
	Customer deposits to total (noninterbank) loans
	Foreign currency-denominated loans to total loans
	Foreign currency-denominated liabilities to total liabilities
	Net open position in equities to capital
Market liquidity	Average bid-ask spread in the securities market[1]
	Average daily turnover ratio in the securities market[1]
Nonbank financial institutions	Assets to total financial system assets
	Assets to GDP
Corporate sector	Total debt to equity
	Return on equity (earnings before interest and taxes to average equity)
	Earnings before interest and taxes to interest and principal expenses
	Corporate net foreign exchange exposure to equity
	Number of applications for protection from creditors
Households	Household debt to GDP
	Household debt service and principal payments to income
Real estate markets	Real estate prices
	Residential real estate loans to total loans
	Commercial real estate loans to total loans

---

[1]Or, in other markets that are most relevant to bank liquidity, such as foreign exchange markets.

---

the indicators identified above. The *Guide* will provide both definitions of, and compilation guidance for, FSIs, particularly the core set.

- Indicators of nonbank financial institutions and markets need to be developed that reflect the specificities of each market segment—finance companies, securities firms, collective investment schemes, insurance companies, and others. Market liquidity indicators are also important and need to be uniformly defined and regularly collected.

- With regard to the corporate sector, while it is possible to identify a set of useful indicators, data availability remains a key obstacle, both at the aggregated and disaggregated level, and particularly for nonlisted companies, which are a significant share of the sector in many countries.

- Efforts to develop better indicators of financial institutions' exposure to the household and real estate sectors should be stepped up, notably in the direction of more transparent information on credit outstanding to these sectors.

- Analytical tools that use FSIs need to be further developed, including more refined methods of aggregate stress testing of financial systems.

- The development of benchmarks for the level of FSIs would help to monitor and interpret developments in the financial system. In particular, guidance would be useful to help to determine the relevant threshold that makes the level of, or change in, an indicator a source for concern. A high degree of flexibility is required in the use of benchmarks, as they are most often country-specific and can change over time.

Monitoring and analysis of FSIs are just one element in an overall assessment of financial stability. Other elements include analyses of macroeconomic developments, market-based data such as stock prices and credit ratings, structural information on the financial sector, and—last, but not least—qualitative assessments, in particular assessments of observance of relevant international standards and codes. These elements, which feed into macroprudential analysis, will help to identify various dimensions of risks as well as the capacity of the system to cope with and manage these risks, thereby helping to form a judgment on overall financial stability. Although these tools still remain imperfect and continue to evolve, macroprudential analysis can reduce the incidence of crises by providing national authorities with a set of tools to comprehensively assess their financial sectors and identify weaknesses at an early stage.

References

Agénor, Pierre R., Joshua Aizenman, and Alexander Hoffmaister, 2000, "The Credit Crunch in East Asia: What Can Bank Excess Liquid Assets Tell?" NBER Working Paper No. 7951 (Cambridge, Massachusetts: National Bureau of Economic Research).

Baldwin, Barbara, and Angeliki Kourelis, forthcoming, "Consolidated Supervision" (Washington: International Monetary Fund).

Ball, Ray, 2001, "Infrastructure Requirement for an Economically Efficient System of Public Financial Reporting and Disclosure," in *Brookings—Wharton Papers on Financial Services 2001*, ed. by Robert E. Litian and Richard Herring (Washington: Brookings Institution).

Barnhill, Theodore M., Panagiotis Papapanagiotou, and Liliana Schumacher, 2000, "Measuring Integrated Market and Credit Risks in Bank Portfolios: An Application to a Set of Hypothetical Banks Operating in South Africa," IMF Working Paper 00/212 (Washington: International Monetary Fund).

Basel Committee on Banking Supervision, 1988, *International Convergence of Capital Measurements and Capital Standards* (Basel: Bank for International Settlements).

———, 1997, "Principles for the Management of Interest Rate Risk," Publication No. 29 (Basel: Bank for International Settlements).

———, 1998, *Amendment to the Capital Accord to Incorporate Market Risks* (Basel: Bank for International Settlements, updated ed.).

———, 2001, *The New Basel Capital Accord* (Basel: Bank for International Settlements).

———, and IOSCO, 1998, "Supervisory Information Framework for Derivatives and Trading Activities," Publication No. 39 (Basel: Bank for International Settlements).

Begum, Jahanara, May Khamis, and Kal Wajid, forthcoming, "Usefulness of Sectoral Balance Sheet Information for Assessing Financial System Vulnerabilities" (Washington: International Monetary Fund).

Berg, Andrew, Eduardo Borensztein, Gian Maria Milesi-Ferretti, and Catherine Patillo, 1999, *Anticipating Balance of Payments Crises: The Role of Early Warning Systems,* IMF Occasional Paper No. 186 (Washington: International Monetary Fund).

Bernanke, Ben S., and Mark Gertler, 1995, "Inside the Black Box: The Credit Channel of Monetary Policy Transmission," NBER Working Paper No. 5146 (Cambridge, Massachusetts: National Bureau of Economic Research).

Blaschke, Winfrid, Matthew Jones, Giovanni Majnoni, and Soledad Martinez Peria, 2001, "Stress Testing of Financial Systems: An Overview of Issues, Methodologies, and FSAP Experiences," IMF Working Paper 01/88 (Washington: International Monetary Fund).

Bloem, Adrian M., 2001, *Quarterly National Accounts Manual* (Washington: International Monetary Fund).

Borio, Claudio, Craig Furfine, and Philip Lowe, 2001, "Procyclicality of the Financial System and Financial Stability: Issues and Policy Options," in *Marrying the Macro- and Micro-Prudential Dimensions of Financial Stability,* BIS Papers No. 1 (Basel: Bank for International Settlements).

Breuer, Peter, 2000, "Measuring Off-Balance Sheet Leverage," IMF Working Paper 00/202 (Washington: International Monetary Fund).

Caballero, Ricardo J., and Arvind Krishnamurthy, 2000, "International and Domestic Collateral Constraints in a Model of Emerging Market Crises," NBER Working Paper No. 7971 (Cambridge, Massachusetts: National Bureau of Economic Research).

Carson, Carol S., 2001, "Toward a Framework for Assessing Data Quality," IMF Working Paper No. 01/25 (Washington: International Monetary Fund).

Céspedes, Luis Felipe, Roberto Chang, and Andrés Velasco, 2000, "Balance Sheets and Exchange Rate Policy," NBER Working Paper No. 7840 (Cambridge, Massachusetts: National Bureau of Economic Research).

Chai, Jingqing, and R. Barry Johnston, 2000, "An Incentive Approach to Identifying Financial Systems Vulnerabilities," IMF Working Paper 00/211 (Washington: International Monetary Fund).

Committee on the Global Financial System, 1999, "Market Liquidity: Research Findings and Selected Policy Implications," Publication No. 11 (Basel: Bank for International Settlements).

———, 2000, "Stress Testing by Large Financial Institutions: Current Practice and Aggregation Issues," Publication No. 14 (Basel: Bank for International Settlements).

———, 2001, "A Survey of Stress Tests and Current Practice at Major Financial Institutions," Publication No. 18 (Basel: Bank for International Settlements).

Cortavarría, Luis, Claudia Dziobek, Akihiro Kanaya, and Inwon Song, 2000, "Loan Review, Provisioning, and Macroeconomic Linkages," IMF Working Paper 00/195 (Washington: International Monetary Fund).

Delgado, Fernando, Daniel Kanda, Greta Mitchell Casselle, and Armando Morales, 2000, "Banks' Domestic Lending in Foreign Currency," MAE Operational Paper 00/4 (Washington: International Monetary Fund).

De Ruiter, Marcel, and David J.C. Smant, 1999, "The Household Balance Sheet and Durable Consumer Expenditures: An Empirical Investigation for The Netherlands, 1972–93," *Journal of Policy Modeling* (U.S.), Vol. 21 (March), pp. 243–74.

Di Pasquale, Denise, and William Wheaton, 1996, *Urban Economics and Real Estate Markets* (Englewood Cliffs: Prentice Hall).

Dziobek, Claudia, J. Kim Hobbs, and David Marston, 2000, "Toward a Framework for Systemic Liquidity Policy," IMF Working Paper 00/34 (Washington: International Monetary Fund).

Evans, Owen, Alfredo M. Leone, Mahinder Gill, and Paul Hilbers, 2000, *Macroprudential Indicators of Financial System Soundness,* IMF Occasional Paper No. 192 (Washington: International Monetary Fund).

Financial Stability Forum, 2001, *Final Report of the Multidisciplinary Working Group on Enhanced Disclosure of the Financial Stability Forum* (Basel: Bank for International Settlements).

Fitch IBCA, 1998, *Corporate Rating Methodology*, August (New York).

Gertler, Mark, Simon Gilchrist, and Fabio Massimo Natalucci, 2000, "External Constraints on Monetary Policy and the Financial Accelerator," paper prepared for the Riksbank Conference on Financial Stability, Stockholm, June.

Gray, Dale F., 1999, "Assessment of Corporate Sector Value and Vulnerability: Links to Exchange Rate and Financial Crises," World Bank Technical Paper No. 455 (Washington: World Bank).

Hilbers, Paul, 2001, "The IMF/World Bank Financial Sector Assessment Program," *Economic Perspectives,* Vol. 6 (February). Available via the Internet: http://www.imf.org/external/np/vc/2001/022301.htm

———, Qin Lei, and Lisbeth Zacho, 2001, "Real Estate Market Developments and Financial Sector Soundness," IMF Working Paper 01/129 (Washington: International Monetary Fund).

International Monetary Fund, 2000a, *World Economic Outlook, May 2000: A Survey by the Staff of the International Monetary Fund,* World Economic and Financial Surveys (Washington).

———, 2000b, *International Capital Markets: Developments, Prospects, and Key Policy Issues* (Washington).

———, 2000c, *Third Review of the IMF's Data Standard Initiatives.* Available via the Internet: http://www.imf.org/external/np/sta/dsbb/2000/index.htm

———, 2000d, *Debt- and Reserve-Related Indicators of External Vulnerability,* Public Information Notice No. 00/37. Available via the Internet: http://www.imf.org/external/np/sec/pn/2000/pn0037.htm

———, 2000e, *Offshore Financial Centers—IMF Background Paper.* Available via the Internet: http://www.imf.org/ external/np/mae/oshore/2000/eng/back.htm

———, 2000f, *Monetary and Financial Statistics Manual* (Washington). Also available via the Internet: http://www.imf.org/external/pubs/ft/mfs/manual

———, 2001a, *IMF Reviews Experience with the Financial Sector Assessment Program (FSAP) and Reaches Conclusions on Issues Going Forward,* Public Information Notice No. 01/11. Available via the Internet: http://www.imf.org/external/np/sec/pn/2001/pn0111.htm

———, 2001b, *Financial Sector Assessment Program (FSAP): A Review: Lessons from the Pilot and Issues Going Forward.* Available via the Internet: http://www.imf.org/external/np/fsap/2001/review.htm

———, 2001c, *Standards and Codes—The IMF's Role,* IMF Issues Brief. Available via the Internet: http://www.imf.org/external/np/exr/ib/2001/042701.htm

Jácome, Luis, and Pamela Madrid, forthcoming, "Bank Restructuring and Central Banks in Latin America" (Washington: International Monetary Fund).

Johnston, R. Barry, Jingqing Chai, and Liliana Schumacher, 2000, "Assessing Financial System Vulnerabilities," IMF Working Paper 00/76 (Washington: International Monetary Fund).

Kim, Se-Jik, and Mark R. Stone, 1999, "Corporate Leverage and Output Adjustment in Post-Crisis East Asia," IMF Working Paper 99/143 (Washington: International Monetary Fund).

Kiyotaki, Nobuhiro, and John Moore, 1997, "Credit Cycles," *Journal of Political Economy*, Vol. 105, No. 21, pp. 211–48.

Krugman, Paul, 1999, "Balance Sheets, the Transfer Problem, and Financial Crises." Available via the Internet: http://web.mit.edu/krugman/www/disinter.html

Moody's Investors Service, 1998, "Industrial Company Rating Methodology," July (New York). Also available via the Internet: http://www.uic.edu/classes/actg/actg516mpb/Homework/Risk/Moody's%methodology.pdf

———, 2000, "Putting EBITDA in Perspective: Ten Critical Failings of EBITDA as the Principal Determinant of Cash Flow," Special Comment, June (New York).

Murphy, Robert G., 1998, "Household Debt and Consumer Spending," *Business Economics*, Vol. 33 (July), pp. 38–42.

Nelson, William, and Wayne Passmore, 2001, "Pragmatic Monitoring of Financial Systems," in *Marrying the Macro- and Micro-Prudential Dimensions of Financial Stability,* BIS Papers No. 1 (Basel: Bank for International Settlements).

Office of the Superintendent of Financial Institutions, 1999, *Supervisory Framework* (Ottawa).

Rajan, Raghuram, and Luigi Zingales, 1995, "What Do We Know about Capital Structure? Some Evidence from International Data," *Journal of Finance*, Vol. 50, No. 5, pp. 1421–60.

Saunders, Anthony, 2000, *Financial Institutions Management: A Modern Perspective* (Boston: Irwin/McGraw-Hill, 3rd ed.).

Schinasi, Garry J., Sean Craig, Burkhard Drees, and Charles Kramer, 2000, *Modern Banking and OTC Derivatives Markets: The Transformation of Global Finance and Its Implications for Systemic Risk*, IMF Occasional Paper No. 203 (Washington: International Monetary Fund).

Standard and Poor's, 2000, *Corporate Ratings Criteria* (New York).

Stone, Mark R., and Melvyn Weeks, 2001, "Systemic Financial Crises, Balance Sheets, and Model Uncertainty," IMF Working Paper 01/162 (Washington: International Monetary Fund).

Sundararajan, Vasuderan, 1999, "Prudential Supervision, Bank Restructuring, and Financial Sector Reform," in *Sequencing Financial Sector Reforms: Country Experiences and Issues,* ed. by R. Barry Johnston and V. Sundararajan (Washington: International Monetary Fund).

———, David D. Marston, and Ritu Basu, 2001, "Financial System Standards and Financial Stability: The Case of Basel Core Principles," IMF Working Paper 01/62 (Washington: International Monetary Fund).

Vittas, Dimitri, 1991, "Measuring Commercial Bank Efficiency: Use and Misuse of Bank Operating Ratios," Policy Research Working Paper No. 806 (Washington: World Bank).

Appendix I   Explanation of FSI Terms

This explanation of indicators included in the core set and the encouraged set of FSIs is provided to clarify this paper's discussion. The terms may not correspond precisely to official defin-itions or standards. The *Compilation Guide on Financial Soundness Indicators* will clarify the definitions of the indicators included in Table A1.1 below.

Table A1.1. Explanation of FSI Terms

Depository Corporations (Core Set)	
Regulatory capital to risk-weighted assets	Capital as defined in the 1988 Capital Accord of the Basel Committee on Banking Supervision (and revisions) divided by risk-weighted assets. Capital is defined using regulatory standards and does not correspond directly to capital as shown in financial balance sheets. Risk-weighted assets equal the sum of each category of asset (and on-balance-sheet equivalents of off-balance-sheet positions) multiplied by a weight representing the credit risk associated with each category.
Regulatory tier 1 capital to risk-weighted assets	The Capital Accord (and revisions) defines three capital elements: tier 1—permanent shareholders' equity and disclosed reserves; tier 2—undisclosed reserves, revaluation reserves, general provisions and loan-loss reserves, hybrid debt-equity capital instruments, and subordinated long-term debt (over five years); and tier 3—subordinated debt (over two years original maturity).
Nonperforming loans to total gross loans	Designed to capture the share of "problem" loans in the total loan portfolio. There is no standard definition of NPLs. In some countries, a loan is considered to be nonperforming when the principal and/or interest payments on it according to the original terms of the loan agreement are past due (e.g., by 90 days or more). Gross loans are used as the denominator as opposed to net loans, which deduct specific provisions (loan-loss reserves) from loans.
Nonperforming loans net of provisions to capital	Compares NPLs and capital. NPLs are net of specific provisions (loan-loss reserves).
Sectoral distribution of loans to total loans[1]	Key sectors may include a dominant commodity export, or other sectors. Classification according to national accounts classifications is encouraged.
Large exposures to capital	Exposure refers to one or more credits to the same individual/economic group. There is no standard definition of "large." In some countries, it refers to exposures exceeding 10 percent of regulatory capital.
Return on assets	Measures banks' efficiency in using their assets. Can be calculated as net income (gross income less noninterest expenses) to average total assets.
Return on equity	Measures banks' efficiency in using their capital. Can be calculated as net income to period average capital.
Interest margin to gross income	Looks at profitability resulting from banks' interest earning assets minus interest expenses—that is, interest margin (or net interest income).
Noninterest expenses to gross income	Compares administrative expenses and gross income (interest margin plus noninterest income).

Table A1.1 *(continued)*

Depository Corporations (Encouraged Set)

Liquid assets to total assets (liquid asset ratio)	Liquid assets, in general, refer to cash and assets that are readily convertible to cash without significant loss, often including government and central bank securities.
Liquid assets to short-term liabilities	Designed to capture the liquidity mismatch of assets and liabilities. A variety of definitions are used at present.
Duration of assets Duration of liabilities	Weighted average term-to-maturity of an asset's (liability's) cash flow, the weights being the present value of each future cash flow as a percent of the asset's full price. Alternative measures of interest rate sensitivity include: (1) average interest rate repricing period for assets and liabilities (period until financial instruments are redeemed or the interest rates on them are reset or reindexed); and (2) average maturity of assets and liabilities. A currency breakdown of duration helps to identify maturity mismatches in foreign currency.
Net open position in foreign exchange to capital	Net on-balance-sheet and off-balance-sheet asset and liability positions in foreign currencies. According to the Basel Committee, net open positions in each currency should be calculated as the sum of net spot position, net forward position, guarantees, net future income and expenses not yet accrued but already fully hedged, net notional value of foreign currency options, and any other item representing a profit/loss in foreign currencies.
Capital to assets	Simple ratio of capital to total assets, without risk weighting. This is the inverse of the leverage ratio.
Geographical distribution of loans to total loans[1]	Loan exposure by foreign country or region.
Gross asset position in derivatives to capital Gross liability position in derivatives to capital	The on-balance-sheet value of derivatives in an asset (or liability) position, plus the fair value of off-balance-sheet derivatives in an asset (or liability) position.
Trading income to total income	Designed to capture the share of banks' income from trading activities, including currency trading.
Personnel expenses to noninterest expenses	Measures the incidence of personnel costs in total administrative costs.
Spread between reference lending and deposit rates	A simple measure of bank profitability as well as of efficiency and competition in financial markets, it measures the difference (usually in basis points) between representative rates. There is no standard definition of reference rates.
Spread between highest and lowest interbank rate	Designed to capture banks' own perception of problems facing banks with access to the interbank market.
Customer deposits to total (noninterbank) loans	A simple measure of liquidity, it compares deposits to loans (excluding interbank activity).
FX-denominated loans to total loans[1] FX-denominated liabilities to total liabilities	These indicators measure the relative size of these exposures.
Net open position in equities to capital	Positions in each equity should be calculated as the sum of on-balance-sheet holdings of equities and notional positions in equity derivatives.

Market Liquidity

Average bid-ask spread in the securities market	A measure of market tightness (the difference between prices at which a market participant is willing to buy and sell a security). The specific market can be that for Treasury bills and bonds, central bank bills, or other securities, depending on the particular conditions in the country.
Average daily turnover ratio in the securities market	As a measure of market depth, it is the volume of securities traded daily as a percentage of total securities listed on an exchange. The indicator could be calculated for a variety of markets.

Table A1.1 *(concluded)*

<table>
<tr><td colspan="2" align="center">Nonbank Financial Intermediaries</td></tr>
<tr><td>NBFI assets to total financial system assets</td><td>Captures the relative importance of NBFIs in a country's total financial assets. It can be broken down by NBFI subsector.</td></tr>
<tr><td>NBFI assets to GDP</td><td>Indicates the relative size of NBFIs in the economy. It can be broken down by NBFI subsector.</td></tr>
<tr><td colspan="2" align="center">Nonbank Nonfinancial Corporations</td></tr>
<tr><td>Total debt to equity</td><td>A measure of corporate leverage, it can be calculated as total debt to book value of equity.</td></tr>
<tr><td>Return on equity</td><td>Captures firms' efficiency in using their equity. Can be calculated as EBIT (earnings before interest and taxes) to average equity.</td></tr>
<tr><td>Debt service coverage</td><td>Measures firms' capacity to cover their debt service payments. Can be calculated as EBIT to interest and principal expenses.</td></tr>
<tr><td>Corporate net FX exposure to equity</td><td>Looks at firms' exposure to foreign exchange risk. It can be calculated as the sum of net positions in each foreign currency.</td></tr>
<tr><td>Number of applications for protection from creditors</td><td>A measure of bankruptcy trends; it is influenced by the quality and nature of bankruptcy and related legislation.</td></tr>
<tr><td colspan="2" align="center">Households</td></tr>
<tr><td>Household debt to GDP</td><td>Captures the overall level of household indebtedness (commonly related to consumer loans and mortgages) as a share of GDP.</td></tr>
<tr><td>Household debt burden to income</td><td>Measures households' capacity to cover their debt payments (principal and interest). Can be calculated as a share of total disposable income.</td></tr>
<tr><td colspan="2" align="center">Real Estate Markets</td></tr>
<tr><td>Real estate prices</td><td>Designed to capture price trends in the real estate market. There is no standard definition and various intracountry and subsectoral breakdowns are possible (e.g., industrial, commercial, retail, and residential).</td></tr>
<tr><td>Residential real estate loans to total loans</td><td>Measures banks' exposure to the real estate sector, with a focus on household borrowers. There is no standard definition. May include mortgage lending and/or other loans collateralized by residential real estate.</td></tr>
<tr><td>Commercial real estate loans to total loans</td><td>Measures banks' exposure to the real estate sector, with a focus on corporate borrowers. There is no standard definition. May include loans for the purchase of commercial real estate, loans to construction companies, and/or other loans collateralized by commercial real estate.</td></tr>
</table>

[1]Data on credit, which is a more comprehensive concept than loans, can be used as an alternative to loans. Credit (assets for which the counterparty incurs debt liabilities) includes loans, securities other than shares, and miscellaneous receivables.

Appendix II   Aggregation Issues

Simple aggregation of balance sheets and income statements of individual institutions can disguise important structural information, and it is often necessary to supplement the aggregate data with information on dispersion. For example, the capital to asset ratio of a system is calculated by dividing the total capital by total assets, which is essentially the average (or mean) capital to asset ratio of the system. If capital asset ratios were symmetrically distributed, this statistic would also convey information about the middle capital asset ratio (the median) as well as the most frequently observed capital asset ratio (the mode). However, typically the distribution is not symmetric; hence, focusing on the mean values only may be misleading as the mean can be affected by value of outliers—for example, one very strongly capitalized bank could be more than offsetting many other undercapitalized banks.

Descriptive statistics on data dispersion provide ways to supplement mean values with additional information. Data skewness can be particularly useful, as it provides a measure of the size and direction of asymmetry in the distribution of the observations. Positive skewness indicates that aggregation biases the results upwards (a substantial number of institutions are actually below the average), and the opposite is true for negative skewness. Skewness is zero when the distribution is symmetrical—that is, mean, median, and mode are equal. To get a sense of the proportional effect of the outliers, or the thickness of the tails, the kurtosis can also be calculated. Ways to calculate the direction and degree of skewness and the degree of kurtosis are discussed below.

Descriptive Statistics and Data Dispersion

Summary measures for a data set are often referred to as descriptive statistics. Descriptive statistics fall into four main categories: (1) measures of position, (2) measures of variability, (3) measures of skewness, and (4) measures of kurtosis. They can be useful for beginning data analysis, for comparing multiple data sets, and for reporting final results of a survey.

Measures of position (or central tendency) describe where the data are concentrated:

- *Mean* (first moment of the distribution, or $\bar{x}$) is the mathematical average of the data and is a common measure of central tendency.

- *Median* (Med) is the middle observation in a data set. The median is often used when a data set is not symmetrical, or when there are outlying observations.

- *Mode* is the value around which the greatest number of observations are concentrated, or the most common observation.

Measures of variability describe the dispersion (or spread) of the data set:

- *Range* is the difference between the largest and the smallest observations in the data set. The range has limitations because it depends on only two numbers in the data set.

- *Variance* (second moment of the distribution, or σ^2) measures the dispersion of the distribution around the mean, taking into account all data points.

- *Standard Deviation* (or σ) is the positive square root of the variance, and is the most common measure of variability. Standard deviation indicates how close to the mean the observations are.

Measures of skewness indicate whether the data are symmetrically distributed:

- *Skewness* (third moment of the distribution, or μ_3) measures the degree of asymmetry of the data set. Positive skewness indicates a longer right-hand side (tail) of the distribution; negative skewness a longer tail on the left. Distributions that are symmetric have identical tails and thus no skewness. One easy way of determining skewness is to compare the values of mean and the median relative to the standard deviation:

$$\gamma = \frac{\bar{x} - Med}{\sigma_x}$$

A more precise method to calculate skewness is the Pearson coefficient:

$$\frac{\mu^3}{\sigma^3} = \frac{\displaystyle\sum_{i=1}^{n}\frac{(x_i - \bar{x})^3 \cdot n_i}{N}}{\sigma_x^3}$$

Measures of kurtosis indicate whether the data are more or less concentrated toward the center:

• *Kurtosis* (fourth moment of the distribution, or μ_4) measures the degree of flatness of the distri-

bution near its center, or equivalently the degree of thickness of the tails. It is large if the distribution has sizeable tails that extend much further from the mean than $\pm \sigma$; kurtosis is zero if the distribution is normal. A normalized measure is:

$$K = \frac{\mu^4}{\sigma^4} = \frac{\displaystyle\sum_{i=1}^{n}\frac{(x_i - \bar{x})^4 \cdot n_i}{N}}{\sigma_x^4} - 3$$

Appendix III Additional FSIs Identified by Respondents

The *User Questionnaire* asked respondents to indicate FSIs not covered in the survey that they consider useful, or FSIs they use that differ from those in the survey. Respondents identified a relatively small number of additional FSIs. Conversely, few commented that the list of FSIs was too long.

As already noted in the body of the paper, additional asset price information (real estate, equities, and bank equities) was requested most often, and a number of respondents identified information on the distribution of observations as being useful.

Some of the other additional FSIs identified are listed below.

- Aggregate growth indicators for various types of lending;

- Distribution of loans by size of borrower;

- Indicators of the composition of liabilities (subordinated debt, guarantees, government credits, etc.);

- Turnover and spreads in securities repo and swaps markets;

- Number of banks and total assets by CAMELS ranking;

- Ratings of banks and their distribution;

- More quickly available "flash indicators," such as bank and bond yields, that provide current assessments of markets;

- Developments in payments systems, including collateral held and liquidity.

Other observations by respondents

Respondents made a number of other observations regarding FSIs and their compilation and dissemination.

- One concern expressed was that aggregation of information on individual financial institutions could result in the offsetting of positions of individual units that could obscure the meaning of some FSIs.

- Several respondents said that regular compilation of a large range of FSIs might not justify the resource costs. One respondent said that financial institutions were already subject to substantial data reporting requirements and would not welcome new statistical demands. It was suggested that ad hoc compilation of FSIs could be carried out when needed.

- Several respondents said that many organizations were working on financial stability issues or closely related initiatives. Close cooperation among parties working in the field was considered desirable.

- One respondent suggested that the selection of FSIs might wait until the completion of the Basel Committee's work on the new capital adequacy framework.

- Several comments were made regarding the proper treatment of money market mutual funds and whether they should be included within the depository corporations sector, as done in the survey. It was noted that the risks faced by money market mutual funds could significantly differ from those faced by banking institutions and therefore mutual funds might be excluded from the analysis or might be separately analyzed. Alternatively, it was suggested that all mutual funds should have been covered in the survey because the greatest risks are likely to be faced by non-money market funds that tended to escape supervision by bank supervisors.

- Several countries commented that flexibility should be sought in presentation of macroprudential information. One G-7 country commented that, "It is not possible to have uniform rules on the presentation of macroprudential indicators. At any rate, caution is advised in view of the heterogeneity that may exist in terms of national concepts and calculation methods."

Appendix IV   Tables of Survey Results

Table A4.1. FSIs for which Components Are Extensively Compiled
(Very useful FSIs—Group I—are in italics)

1.1	*Basel capital adequacy ratio*
1.1a	*Ratio of Basel tier I capital to risk-weighted assets*
1.1b	Ratio of Basel tier I + tier II capital to risk-weighted assets
1.3	Ratio of total on-balance-sheet assets to own funds
2.1	Distribution of on-balance-sheet assets by Basel risk category
2.4	*Distribution of loans by sector*
2.4b	Loans for investment in residential real estate
2.5	*Distribution of credit extended by sector*
2.6	Distribution of credit, by country or region
2.7	Ratio of credit to related entities to total credit
2.8	*Ratio of total large loans to own funds*
2.9	*Ratio of gross nonperforming assets to total assets*
2.10	*Ratio of nonperforming loans net of provisions to total assets*
3.1	Change in the number of depository corporations
3.2	*Ratio of profits to period-average assets (ROA)*
3.3	*Ratio of profits to period-average equity (ROE)*
3.4	*Ratio of net interest income to profits*
3.5	Ratio of trading and foreign currency gains/losses to profits
3.6	Ratio of operating costs to net interest income
3.7	Ratio of staff costs to operating costs
3.8	*Spread between reference lending and deposit rates*
3.9	Share of assets of the three largest depository corporations in total assets of depository corporations
4.3	*Ratio of liquid assets to total assets*
4.4	*Ratio of liquid assets to liquid liabilities*
4.9	Ratio of central bank credit to depository corporations to their total liabilities
4.10	Ratio of total customer deposits to total (noninterbank) loans
4.11	Ratio of foreign currency customer deposits to total (noninterbank) foreign currency loans
5.1	Ratio of gross foreign currency assets to own funds
5.2	Ratio of net foreign currency positions to own funds
5.7	Ratio of gross positions in equities to own funds

Table A4.2. SDDS Subscribers: Compilation and Dissemination of FSIs and Components[1]

FSI		Usefulness Score	Percent Compiling FSIs	Percent Disseminating FSIs	Percent Compiling Components	Percent Disseminating Components
1.	*Capital adequacy*					
1.1	Basel capital adequacy ratio	3.8	78	62	78	62
1.1a	Ratio of Basel tier I capital to risk-weighted assets	3.6	74	48	74	48
1.1b	Ratio of Basel tier I + tier II capital to risk-weighted assets	3.4	76	48	76	48
1.1c	Ratio of Basel tier I + II + III capital to risk-weighted assets	3.0	46	28	46	28
1.2	Distribution of capital adequacy ratios (number of institutions within specified capital adequacy ratio ranges)	3.4	22	8	22	8
1.3	Ratio of total on-balance-sheet assets to own funds	3.1	40	18	80	60
2.	*Asset quality*					
(a)	Lending institutions					
2.1	Distribution of on-balance-sheet assets, by Basel risk-weight category	3.4	76	32	76	32
2.2	Ratio of total gross asset position in financial derivatives to own funds	2.9	28	10	50	16
2.3	Ratio of total gross liability position in financial derivatives to own funds	2.9	24	10	46	16
2.4	Distribution of loans, by sector	3.6	76	64	72	64
2.4a	*of which:* for investment in commercial real estate	3.3	40	32	40	32
2.4b	*of which:* for investment in residential real estate	3.3	56	48	56	48
2.5	Distribution of credit extended, by sector	3.5	48	36	54	42
2.6	Distribution of credit extended, by country or region	3.3	60	44	68	50
2.7	Ratio of credit to related entities to total credit	3.3	24	6	62	16
2.8	Ratio of total large loans to own funds	3.4	28	8	54	16
2.9	Ratio of gross nonperforming loans to total assets	3.9	46	32	80	58
2.10	Ratio of nonperforming loans net of provisions to total assets	3.8	42	24	68	44
(b)	Borrowing institutions					
2.11	Ratio of corporate debt to own funds ("debt-equity ratio")	3.5	24	16	48	36
2.12	Ratio of corporate profits to equity	3.3	22	14	48	36
2.13	Ratio of corporate debt service costs to total corporate income	3.3	22	14	44	28
2.14	Corporate net foreign currency exposure	3.3	4	0	14	6
2.15	Ratio of household total debt to GDP	3.1	22	12	48	34
2.15a	*of which:* mortgage debt to GDP	2.9	38	28	38	28
2.15b	*of which:* debt owed to depository corporations to GDP	2.9	44	36	44	36
2.16	Number of applications for protection from creditors	2.7	22	18	22	18
3.	*Profitability and competitiveness indicators*					
3.1	Rate of change in number of depository corporations	2.6	40	30	60	50
3.3	Ratios of profits to period-average equity (ROE)	3.6	48	42	74	50
3.4	Ratio of net interest income to total income	3.5	44	30	82	64
3.5	Ratio of trading and foreign exchange gains/losses to total income	3.3	36	24	74	54
3.6	Ratio of operating costs to net interest income	3.3	42	26	84	58
3.7	Ratio of staff costs to operating costs	3.1	42	28	82	56
3.8	Spread between reference lending and deposit rates	3.5	22	18	52	48
3.9	Share of assets of the three largest depository corporations in total assets of depository corporations	2.8	38	18	72	32
4.	*Liquidity*					
4.1	Distribution of three-month local currency interbank rates for different depository corporations	2.9	18	8	18	8

Table A4.2 *(concluded)*

FSI		Usefulness Score	Percent Compiling FSIs	Percent Disseminating FSIs	Percent Compiling Components	Percent Disseminating Components
4.2	Average interbank bid-ask spread for three-month local currency deposits	3.0	22	12	22	12
4.3	Ratio of liquid assets to total assets	3.4	40	20	70	34
4.4	Ratio of liquid assets to liquid liabilities	3.4	40	20	68	34
4.5	Average maturity of assets	3.3	16	6	30	14
4.6	Average maturity of liabilities	3.2	16	6	34	14
4.7	Average daily turnover in the treasury bill (or central bank bill) market	2.6	30	20	30	20
4.8	Average bid-ask spread in the treasury bill (or central bank bill) market	2.7	16	6	16	6
4.9	Ratio of central bank credit to depository corporations to depository corporations' total liabilities	2.8	20	14	70	58
4.10	Ratio of customer deposits to total (noninterbank) loans	3.0	36	14	80	66
4.11	Ratio of customer foreign currency deposits to total (noninterbank) foreign currency loans	2.8	26	14	68	48
5.	*Sensitivity to market risk indicators*					
5.1	Ratio of gross foreign currency assets to own funds	3.0	28	10	72	44
5.2	Ratio of net foreign currency position to own funds	3.3	28	10	50	18
5.3	Average interest rate repricing period for assets	3.0	26	2	26	2
5.4	Average interest rate repricing period for liabilities	3.0	26	2	26	2
5.5	Duration of assets	3.2	18	2	18	2
5.6	Duration of liabilities	3.2	18	2	18	2
5.7	Ratio of gross equity position to own funds	2.9	22	10	62	42
5.8	Ratio of net equity position to own funds	2.9	18	10	30	16
5.9	Ratio of gross position in commodities to own funds	2.3	10	4	26	12
5.10	Ratio of net position in commodities to own funds	2.4	14	6	24	10

[1]The denominator used in columns three and five is 50, the total number of SDDS countries as of December 2001.

Table A4.3. Usefulness of FSIs by Type of User and Type of Economy

		Supervisors			
		Industrial	Emerging	Developing	Average
1.	*Capital adequacy*				
1.1	Basel capital adequacy ratio	3.9	3.9	3.8	3.9
1.1a	Ratio of Basel tier I capital to risk-weighted assets	3.8	3.6	3.7	3.7
1.1b	Ratio of Basel tier I + tier II capital to risk-weighted assets	3.4	3.7	3.6	3.6
1.1c	Ratio of Basel tier I + II + III capital to risk-weighted assets	3.1	3.3	3.2	3.2
1.2	Distribution of capital adequacy ratios (number of institutions within specified capital adequacy ratio ranges)	3.3	3.4	3.2	3.3
1.3	Ratio of total on-balance-sheet assets to own funds	2.8	3.3	3.1	3.1
2.	*Asset quality*				
(a)	Lending institutions				
2.1	Distribution of on-balance-sheet assets, by Basel risk-weight category	3.2	3.6	3.5	3.5
2.2	Ratio of total gross asset position in financial derivatives to own funds	2.5	3.0	2.4	2.7
2.3	Ratio of total gross liability position in financial derivatives to own funds	2.5	2.9	2.4	2.7
2.4	Distribution of loans by sector	3.6	3.6	3.5	3.6
2.4a	*of which:* for investment in commercial real estate	3.3	3.3	3.2	3.3
2.4b	*of which:* for investment in residential real estate	3.3	3.3	3.2	3.3
2.5	Distribution of credit extended by sector	3.4	3.6	3.7	3.6
2.6	Distribution of credit extended by country or region	3.3	3.1	2.8	3.1
2.7	Ratio of credit to related entities to total credit	3.1	3.6	3.6	3.5
2.8	Ratio of total large loans to own funds	3.4	3.7	3.7	3.6
2.9	Ratio of gross nonperforming loans to total assets	3.9	3.8	3.9	3.9
2.10	Ratio of nonperforming loans net of provisions to total assets	3.9	3.7	3.8	3.8
(b)	Borrowing institutions				
2.11	Ratio of corporate debt to own funds ("debt-equity ratio")	3.4	3.5	3.3	3.4
2.12	Ratio of corporate profits to equity	3.2	3.4	3.3	3.3
2.13	Ratio of corporate debt service costs to total corporate income	3.3	3.3	3.0	3.2
2.14	Corporate net foreign currency exposure	3.2	3.3	3.1	3.2
2.15	Ratio of household total debt to GDP	3.1	2.8	2.8	2.9
2.15a	*of which:* mortgage debt to GDP	3.0	2.7	2.8	2.8
2.15b	*of which:* debt owed to depository corporations to GDP	3.0	2.7	3.0	2.9
2.16	Number of applications for protection from creditors	2.6	2.8	2.6	2.7
3.	*Profitability and competitiveness*				
3.1	Rate of change in number of depository corporations	2.6	2.7	3.0	2.8
3.2	Ratio of profits to period-average assets (ROA)	3.6	3.8	3.6	3.7
3.3	Ratio of profits to period-average equity (ROE)	3.7	3.7	3.6	3.7
3.4	Ratio of net interest income to total income	3.6	3.6	3.8	3.7
3.5	Ratio of trading and foreign exchange gains/losses to total income	3.5	3.4	3.4	3.4
3.6	Ratio of operating costs to net interest income	3.3	3.6	3.6	3.6
3.7	Ratio of staff costs to operating costs	3.0	3.4	3.5	3.4
3.8	Spread between reference lending and deposit rates	3.5	3.5	3.7	3.6
3.9	Share of assets of the three largest depository corporations in total assets of depository corporations	2.9	3.2	2.9	3.0
4.	*Liquidity*				
4.1	Distribution of three-month local currency interbank rates for different depository corporations	2.7	3.0	2.9	2.9
4.2	Average interbank bid-ask spread for three-month local currency deposits	3.0	2.9	2.9	2.9
4.3	Ratio of liquid assets to total assets	3.3	3.6	3.5	3.5
4.4	Ratio of liquid assets to liquid liabilities	3.3	3.7	3.7	3.6
4.5	Average maturity of assets	3.2	3.3	3.6	3.4
4.6	Average maturity of liabilities	3.2	3.3	3.6	3.4
4.7	Average daily turnover in the Treasury bill (or central bank bill) market	2.3	2.7	3.1	2.7

Type of User											
Policy/Research				Private Sector				Average			
Industrial	Emerging	Developing	Average	Industrial	Emerging	Developing	Average	Industrial	Emerging	Developing	World Total
3.9	3.9	3.2	3.7	3.4	3.8	3.5	3.6	3.7	3.9	3.6	3.8
3.4	3.6	3.2	3.4	3.6	3.6	3.3	3.5	3.6	3.6	3.5	3.6
3.2	3.6	3.1	3.3	3.1	3.3	3.1	3.2	3.2	3.6	3.4	3.4
2.9	3.0	2.8	2.9	2.7	2.9	3.1	2.9	2.9	3.1	3.1	3.0
3.6	3.6	2.9	3.4	3.1	3.1	3.2	3.1	3.3	3.4	3.1	3.3
3.1	3.4	3.5	3.4	3.0	3.1	3.5	3.1	2.9	3.3	3.3	3.2
3.1	3.5	3.2	3.3	3.4	3.4	3.5	3.4	3.2	3.5	3.4	3.4
2.8	3.2	3.0	3.0	2.9	2.7	2.5	2.7	2.7	3.0	2.6	2.8
2.8	3.2	2.9	3.0	2.8	2.7	2.5	2.7	2.7	2.9	2.6	2.8
3.6	3.8	3.5	3.6	3.4	3.4	3.7	3.5	3.5	3.6	3.5	3.6
3.5	3.5	3.1	3.4	3.2	2.9	3.0	3.0	3.3	3.3	3.1	3.2
3.4	3.4	3.1	3.3	3.2	2.9	3.0	3.0	3.3	3.2	3.2	3.2
3.4	3.6	3.6	3.6	3.2	3.7	3.0	3.4	3.3	3.6	3.6	3.5
3.2	3.2	2.7	3.1	3.2	3.4	2.8	3.2	3.2	3.2	2.8	3.1
3.0	3.7	3.3	3.4	2.9	3.5	2.8	3.1	3.0	3.6	3.5	3.4
3.2	3.5	3.5	3.4	3.1	3.3	3.5	3.2	3.2	3.6	3.6	3.5
3.9	4.0	3.8	3.9	3.7	3.9	3.7	3.8	3.9	3.9	3.8	3.9
3.8	3.9	3.6	3.8	3.7	3.7	3.7	3.7	3.8	3.8	3.8	3.8
3.8	3.7	3.3	3.6	3.1	3.4	3.4	3.3	3.4	3.5	3.3	3.4
3.3	3.5	3.2	3.4	2.9	3.2	3.1	3.1	3.1	3.4	3.2	3.3
3.3	3.5	3.1	3.3	2.8	3.3	2.7	3.0	3.2	3.4	3.0	3.2
3.2	3.5	2.6	3.2	3.2	3.5	2.7	3.3	3.2	3.4	2.9	3.2
3.5	3.2	2.9	3.2	3.1	2.9	2.5	2.9	3.2	3.0	2.8	3.0
3.3	2.9	2.8	3.0	2.9	2.7	2.3	2.7	3.1	2.8	2.7	2.8
3.1	3.0	2.8	3.0	2.9	2.8	2.3	2.7	3.0	2.8	2.8	2.9
3.1	2.6	2.6	2.8	2.8	2.7	2.0	2.6	2.8	2.7	2.5	2.7
2.5	2.7	2.7	2.6	1.9	2.9	3.1	2.6	2.4	2.7	2.9	2.7
3.5	3.8	3.5	3.6	3.1	3.7	3.6	3.5	3.5	3.8	3.6	3.6
3.6	3.9	3.5	3.7	2.9	3.7	3.6	3.4	3.5	3.8	3.6	3.6
3.2	3.7	3.1	3.4	3.0	3.6	3.4	3.3	3.3	3.6	3.6	3.5
3.1	3.4	2.8	3.2	2.9	3.4	3.3	3.2	3.2	3.4	3.3	3.3
3.0	3.6	3.5	3.4	2.6	3.5	3.3	3.1	3.0	3.6	3.6	3.4
2.7	3.4	3.0	3.1	2.5	3.3	3.3	3.0	2.8	3.4	3.4	3.2
3.4	3.7	3.5	3.5	3.2	3.6	2.9	3.3	3.4	3.6	3.5	3.5
2.6	3.2	2.9	2.9	2.5	2.9	2.8	2.7	2.7	3.1	2.9	2.9
2.6	3.1	2.9	2.9	2.9	3.1	2.4	2.9	2.7	3.1	2.8	2.9
2.6	3.1	2.7	2.8	3.0	3.2	2.3	2.9	2.9	3.0	2.7	2.9
3.1	3.7	3.8	3.5	3.3	3.6	3.3	3.4	3.2	3.6	3.5	3.5
2.9	3.7	3.9	3.5	3.4	3.7	3.3	3.5	3.2	3.7	3.7	3.6
2.9	3.7	3.7	3.4	3.0	3.3	3.4	3.2	3.0	3.4	3.6	3.4
2.9	3.7	3.7	3.4	3.0	3.3	3.4	3.2	3.0	3.4	3.6	3.4
2.1	3.2	3.3	2.9	2.5	3.2	2.7	2.8	2.3	3.0	3.1	2.8

Table A4.3 *(concluded)*

		Supervisors			
		Industrial	Emerging	Developing	Average
4.8	Average bid-ask spread in the Treasury bill (or central bank bill) market	2.3	2.8	2.9	2.7
4.9	Ratio of central bank credit to depository corporations to depository corporations' total liabilities	2.6	3.1	2.9	2.9
4.10	Ratio of customer deposits to total (noninterbank) loans	3.1	3.2	3.5	3.3
4.11	Ratio of customer foreign currency deposits to total (noninterbank) foreign currency loans	2.6	3.1	3.0	3.0
5.	*Sensitivity to market risks*				
5.1	Ratio of gross foreign currency assets to own funds	2.7	3.2	3.2	3.1
5.2	Ratio of net foreign currency position to own funds	3.3	3.7	3.5	3.5
5.3	Average interest rate repricing period for assets	3.0	3.2	3.1	3.1
5.4	Average interest rate repricing period for liabilities	2.9	3.1	3.1	3.1
5.5	Duration of assets	3.0	3.2	3.0	3.1
5.6	Duration of liabilities	3.0	3.1	3.1	3.1
5.7	Ratio of gross equity position to own funds	2.9	2.9	2.8	2.9
5.8	Ratio of net equity position to own funds	2.9	2.9	2.9	2.9
5.9	Ratio of gross position in commodities to own funds	2.3	2.3	2.1	2.2
5.10	Ratio of net position in commodities to own funds	2.3	2.3	2.3	2.3

Type of User											
Policy/Research				Private Sector				Average			
Industrial	Emerging	Developing	Average	Industrial	Emerging	Developing	Average	Industrial	Emerging	Developing	World Total
2.2	3.3	3.2	2.9	2.5	3.2	2.7	2.8	2.3	3.0	3.0	2.8
2.6	3.1	2.6	2.8	2.6	3.0	2.6	2.8	2.6	3.1	2.8	2.9
2.9	3.4	3.0	3.2	2.6	3.2	3.0	2.9	2.9	3.3	3.3	3.2
2.4	3.2	2.8	2.9	2.9	3.1	2.3	2.8	2.6	3.1	2.9	2.9
2.6	3.3	3.2	3.1	2.9	3.1	3.3	3.0	2.7	3.2	3.2	3.1
2.9	3.5	3.5	3.3	3.1	3.5	3.3	3.3	3.1	3.6	3.5	3.4
2.8	3.4	2.8	3.0	2.6	3.3	2.8	2.9	2.8	3.3	3.0	3.0
2.8	3.4	2.8	3.0	2.6	3.3	2.8	2.9	2.8	3.2	3.0	3.0
2.9	3.6	3.0	3.3	3.0	3.4	3.0	3.2	3.0	3.4	3.0	3.2
2.9	3.6	3.0	3.3	3.1	3.3	3.0	3.2	3.0	3.3	3.0	3.2
2.7	3.1	3.3	3.0	2.7	2.9	2.8	2.8	2.8	3.0	3.0	2.9
2.8	3.1	3.4	3.1	2.7	2.8	3.0	2.8	2.8	3.0	3.1	3.0
2.3	2.7	2.7	2.6	2.3	2.5	2.5	2.4	2.3	2.5	2.4	2.4
2.4	2.7	2.8	2.6	2.3	2.5	2.5	2.4	2.3	2.5	2.5	2.4

Table A4.4. Compilation and Dissemination of FSIs by Type of Economy

	Industrial Countries				
	Total in Group	Number Compiling FSIs	Percent of Total	Number Disseminating FSIs	Percent of Total
1. *Capital adequacy*					
1.1 Basel capital adequacy ratio	21	20	95	15	71
a. Basel tier I capital (net of deductions)	21	19	90	13	62
b. Basel tier II capital (net of deductions)	21	19	90	12	57
c. Basel tier III capital (net of deductions)	21	15	71	8	38
d. Risk-weighted assets	21	19	90	12	57
1.2 Distribution of capital adequacy ratios	21	8	38	3	14
a. Number of institutions with Basel capital ratios, falling into specified ranges	21	8	38	3	14
b. Assets of institutions within each range	21	12	57	6	29
c. Assets by type of depository corporation					
c.1 Headquartered in the country	21	13	62	5	24
of which: internationally active	21	7	33	2	10
of which: state-owned or -controlled	21	7	33	3	14
c.2 Headquartered in other countries	21	11	52	2	10
1.3 Ratio of total on-balance-sheet assets to own funds	21	13	62	6	29
a. Total on-balance-sheet assets	21	20	95	13	62
b. Own funds (equity capital and reserves)	21	20	95	13	62
2. *Asset quality*					
(a) Lending institution					
2.1 Distribution of on-balance-sheet assets by Basel risk-weight category	21	17	81	7	33
a. Assets per Basel risk-weight category	21	17	81	7	33
2.2 Ratio of total gross asset position in financial derivatives to own funds	21	9	43	4	19
a. Total gross asset position in derivatives	21	15	71	6	29
b. of which: off-balance-sheet position	21	14	67	4	19
2.3 Ratio of total gross liability position in financial derivatives to own funds	21	7	33	4	19
a. Total gross liability position in derivatives	21	14	67	6	29
b. of which: off-balance-sheet position	21	12	57	4	19
2.4 Distribution of loans by sector	21	21	100	17	81
a. Loans by national accounts sectors	21	20	95	17	81
of which:					
a.1. Loans for investment in commercial real estate	21	13	62	9	43
a.2. Loans for investment in residential real estate	21	17	81	15	71
a.3. Loans to other key sectors (specify)	21	14	67	10	48
b. Total loans	21	19	90	19	90
2.5 Distribution of credit extended by sector	21	11	52	7	33
a. Credit by national account sectors	21	13	62	9	43
b. Total credit	21	18	86	13	62
2.6 Distribution of credit by country or region	21	16	76	12	57
a. Loans by country or region	21	18	86	13	62
2.7 Ratio of credit to related entities to total credit	21	6	29	2	10
a. Credit to related entities	21	13	62	3	14
2.8 Ratio of total large loans to own funds	21	6	29	0	0
a. Total large loans (specify size range)	21	12	57	1	5
2.9 Ratio of gross nonperforming loans to total assets	21	13	62	9	43
a. Gross nonperforming loans	21	19	90	12	57
2.10 Ratio of nonperforming loans net of provisions to total assets	21	12	57	8	38
a. Nonperforming loans net of provisions	21	18	86	11	52
(b) Borrowing institution					
2.11 Ratio of corporate debt to own funds ("debt-equity ratio")	21	9	43	7	33
a. Total corporate debt	21	16	76	12	57
b. Corporations' own funds	21	15	71	12	57

	Emerging Countries					Developing Countries					World Total			
Total in Group	Number Compiling FSIs	Percent of Total	Number Disseminating FSIs	Percent of Total	Total in Group	Number Compiling FSIs	Percent of Total	Number Disseminating FSIs	Percent of Total	Total in Group	Number Compiling FSIs	Percent of Total	Number Disseminating FSIs	Percent of Total
44	38	86	27	61	28	27	96	11	39	93	85	91	53	57
44	37	84	21	48	28	25	89	10	36	93	81	87	44	47
44	36	82	21	48	28	24	86	10	36	93	79	85	43	46
44	14	32	9	20	28	7	25	4	14	93	36	39	21	23
44	41	93	24	55	28	24	86	11	39	93	84	90	47	51
44	7	16	3	7	28	6	21	5	18	93	21	23	11	12
44	7	16	3	7	28	6	21	5	18	93	21	23	11	12
44	15	34	8	18	28	10	36	4	14	93	37	40	18	19
44	13	30	6	14	28	8	29	3	11	93	34	37	14	15
44	11	25	6	14	28	4	14	1	4	93	22	24	9	10
44	14	32	7	16	28	6	21	2	7	93	27	29	12	13
44	12	27	7	16	28	3	11	0	0	93	26	28	9	10
44	17	39	9	20	28	4	14	2	7	93	34	37	17	18
44	38	86	31	70	28	19	68	11	39	93	77	83	55	59
44	38	86	30	68	28	19	68	11	39	93	77	83	54	58
44	39	89	17	39	28	21	75	9	32	93	77	83	33	35
44	39	89	17	39	28	21	75	9	32	93	77	83	33	35
44	5	11	1	2	28	1	4	0	0	93	15	16	5	5
44	14	32	8	18	28	3	11	1	4	93	32	34	15	16
44	14	32	6	14	28	3	11	1	4	93	31	33	11	12
44	5	11	1	2	28	1	4	0	0	93	13	14	5	5
44	14	32	8	18	28	2	7	0	0	93	30	32	14	15
44	15	34	7	16	28	2	7	0	0	93	29	31	11	12
44	34	77	27	61	28	21	75	16	57	93	76	82	60	65
44	29	66	23	52	28	19	68	14	50	93	68	73	54	58
44	14	32	10	23	28	14	50	11	39	93	41	44	30	32
44	19	43	13	30	28	15	54	12	43	93	51	55	40	43
44	24	55	20	45	28	15	54	10	36	93	53	57	40	43
44	36	82	33	75	28	22	79	17	61	93	77	83	69	74
44	22	50	17	39	28	13	46	11	39	93	46	49	35	38
44	24	55	18	41	28	16	57	14	50	93	53	57	41	44
44	33	75	28	64	28	22	79	18	64	93	73	78	59	63
44	19	43	12	27	28	7	25	4	14	93	42	45	28	30
44	22	50	15	34	28	8	29	5	18	93	48	52	33	35
44	12	27	3	7	28	8	29	2	7	93	26	28	7	8
44	32	73	10	23	28	18	64	8	29	93	63	68	21	23
44	15	34	7	16	28	8	29	1	4	93	29	31	8	9
44	26	59	11	25	28	14	50	8	29	93	52	56	20	22
44	20	45	14	32	28	9	32	5	18	93	42	45	28	30
44	39	89	26	59	28	22	79	13	46	93	80	86	51	55
44	17	39	8	18	28	10	36	6	21	93	39	42	22	24
44	31	70	18	41	28	21	75	13	46	93	70	75	42	45
44	5	11	2	5	28	3	11	0	0	93	17	18	9	10
44	14	32	11	25	28	8	29	4	14	93	38	41	27	29
44	13	30	10	23	28	6	21	3	11	93	34	37	25	27

Table A4.4 *(continued)*

	Industrial Countries				
	Total in Group	Number Compiling FSIs	Percent of Total	Number Disseminating FSIs	Percent of Total
2.12 Ratio of corporate profits to equity	21	8	38	6	29
a. Corporate pre-tax profits	21	15	71	12	57
b. Corporate post-tax profits	21	14	67	11	52
2.13 Ratio of corporate debt service costs to profits	21	9	43	7	33
a. Corporate debt service costs	21	15	71	11	52
2.14 Corporate net foreign currency exposure	21	1	5	0	0
a. Gross foreign currency assets	21	5	24	3	14
b. Gross foreign currency liabilities	21	5	24	3	14
c. Net off-balance-sheet foreign currency positions (nominal value) not included above	21	2	10	0	0
2.15 Ratio of household debt to GDP	21	8	38	5	24
a. Household total debt	21	17	81	13	62
b. *of which:* mortgage debt	21	13	62	10	48
c. *of which:* debt to depository corporations	21	14	67	13	62
2.16 Number of applications for protection from creditors	21	9	43	8	38
3. *Profitability and competitiveness*					
3.1 Rate of change in the number of depository corporations	21	14	67	11	52
a. Difference between number of institutions at beginning and end of period	21	19	90	15	71
b. *of which:* due to mergers and acquisitions	21	17	81	10	48
c. *of which:* due to withdrawals of licenses or closing of units	21	17	81	12	57
3.2 Ratios of profits to period-average assets (ROA)	21	13	62	10	48
a. Pretax, after provisions profits	21	19	90	16	76
b. Posttax profits	21	20	95	16	76
c. Total period-average on-balance-sheet assets	21	18	86	13	62
3.3 Ratios of profits to period-average equity (ROE)	21	14	67	11	52
a. Pretax, after provisions profits	21	19	90	15	71
b. Posttax profits	21	20	95	16	76
c. Period-average equity	21	18	86	13	62
3.4 Ratio of net interest income to profits	21	13	62	8	38
a. Net interest income	21	20	95	16	76
3.5 Ratio of trading and foreign currency gains/losses to profits	21	11	52	7	33
a. Gains/losses in securities and foreign currencies	21	18	86	13	62
3.6 Ratio of operating costs to net interest income	21	13	62	8	38
a. Operating costs	21	20	95	16	76
3.7 Ratio of staff costs to operating costs	21	12	57	8	38
a. Staff costs	21	19	90	14	67
3.8 Spreads between reference lending and deposit rates	21	8	38	5	24
a. Reference lending rate (specify rate)	21	13	62	13	62
b. Reference deposit rate (specify rate)	21	13	62	13	62
3.9 Share of assets of the three largest depository corporations in total assets of depository corporations	21	12	57	5	24
a. Assets of the three largest depository corporations	21	19	90	7	33
4. *Liquidity*					
4.1 Distribution of three-month local currency interbank rates for different banks	21	3	14	1	5
4.2 Average interbank bid-ask spread for three-month local currency interbank deposits	21	6	29	3	14
4.3 Ratio of liquid assets to total assets	21	10	48	5	24
a. Liquid assets	21	18	86	7	33
4.4 Ratio of liquid assets to liquid liabilities	21	11	52	5	24
a. Liquid liabilities	21	18	86	7	33

	Emerging Countries					Developing Countries					World Total			
Total in Group	Number Compiling FSIs	Percent of Total	Number Disseminating FSIs	Percent of Total	Total in Group	Number Compiling FSIs	Percent of Total	Number Disseminating FSIs	Percent of Total	Total in Group	Number Compiling FSIs	Percent of Total	Number Disseminating FSIs	Percent of Total
44	4	9	2	5	28	3	11	1	4	93	15	16	9	10
44	17	39	11	25	28	10	36	5	18	93	42	45	28	30
44	16	36	10	23	28	9	32	4	14	93	39	42	25	27
44	3	7	1	2	28	1	4	1	4	93	13	14	9	10
44	11	25	4	9	28	5	18	4	14	93	31	33	19	20
44	3	7	2	5	28	2	7	0	0	93	6	6	2	2
44	11	25	7	16	28	11	39	6	21	93	27	29	16	17
44	11	25	7	16	28	10	36	5	18	93	26	28	15	16
44	9	20	5	11	28	7	25	4	14	93	18	19	9	10
44	4	9	2	5	28	1	4	0	0	93	13	14	7	8
44	11	25	8	18	28	5	18	0	0	93	33	35	21	23
44	9	20	6	14	28	3	11	0	0	93	25	27	16	17
44	13	30	10	23	28	2	7	0	0	93	29	31	23	25
44	3	7	1	2	28	1	4	1	4	93	13	14	10	11
44	13	30	9	20	28	8	29	8	29	93	35	38	28	30
44	26	59	22	50	28	14	50	12	43	93	59	63	49	53
44	26	59	20	45	28	15	54	13	46	93	58	62	43	46
44	26	59	20	45	28	15	54	12	43	93	58	62	44	47
44	19	43	15	34	28	10	36	4	14	93	42	45	29	31
44	38	86	27	61	28	23	82	14	50	93	80	86	57	61
44	40	91	29	66	28	21	75	13	46	93	81	87	58	62
44	39	89	22	50	28	18	64	10	36	93	75	81	45	48
44	20	45	16	36	28	10	36	4	14	93	44	47	31	33
44	36	82	25	57	28	22	79	12	43	93	77	83	52	56
44	40	91	29	66	28	21	75	11	39	93	81	87	56	60
44	38	86	23	52	28	18	64	10	36	93	74	80	46	49
44	18	41	12	27	28	8	29	3	11	93	39	42	23	25
44	39	89	27	61	28	23	82	11	39	93	82	88	54	58
44	14	32	8	18	28	5	18	1	4	93	30	32	16	17
44	29	66	20	45	28	17	61	8	29	93	64	69	41	44
44	17	39	10	23	28	8	29	3	11	93	38	41	21	23
44	39	89	25	57	28	22	79	12	43	93	81	87	53	57
44	17	39	10	23	28	8	29	3	11	93	37	40	21	23
44	37	84	24	55	28	22	79	12	43	93	78	84	50	54
44	8	18	7	16	28	9	32	4	14	93	25	27	16	17
44	29	66	25	57	28	13	46	9	32	93	55	59	47	51
44	27	61	24	55	28	13	46	9	32	93	53	57	46	49
44	17	39	9	20	28	6	21	2	7	93	35	38	16	17
44	37	84	16	36	28	11	39	7	25	93	67	72	30	32
44	13	30	7	16	28	7	25	4	14	93	23	25	12	13
44	9	20	6	14	28	3	11	2	7	93	18	19	11	12
44	19	43	9	20	28	8	29	6	21	93	37	40	20	22
44	34	77	20	45	28	23	82	14	50	93	75	81	41	44
44	18	41	12	27	28	8	29	5	18	93	37	40	22	24
44	33	75	20	45	28	21	75	12	43	93	72	77	39	42

Table A4.4 *(concluded)*

	Industrial Countries				
	Total in Group	Number Compiling FSIs	Percent of Total	Number Disseminating FSIs	Percent of Total
4.5 Average maturity of assets	21	3	14	0	0
a. Average remaining maturity of assets (months)	21	8	38	1	5
b. *of which:* foreign currency assets	21	6	29	1	5
c. Average original maturity of assets (months)	21	4	19	1	5
d. *of which:* foreign currency assets	21	4	19	0	0
4.6 Average maturity of liabilities	21	3	14	0	0
a. Average remaining maturity of liabilities (months)	21	8	38	1	5
b. *of which:* foreign currency liabilities	21	6	29	1	5
c. Average original maturity of liabilities (months)	21	4	19	1	5
d. *of which:* foreign currency liabilities	21	4	19	0	0
4.7 Average daily turnover in the Treasury bill (or central bank bill) market	21	7	33	4	19
4.8 Average bid-ask spread in the Treasury bill (or central bank bill) market	21	3	14	0	0
4.9 Ratio of central bank credit to depository corporations to their total liabilities	21	6	29	4	19
a. Total credit from the central bank to depository corporations	21	18	86	14	67
b. Total liabilities	21	18	86	14	67
4.10 Ratio of total customer deposits to total (noninterbank) loans	21	11	52	4	19
a. Customer (noninterbank) deposits	21	19	90	15	71
b. Total (noninterbank) loans	21	19	90	15	71
4.11 Ratio of foreign currency customer deposits to total (noninterbank) foreign currency loans	21	7	33	4	19
a. Customer (noninterbank) foreign currency deposits	21	16	76	12	57
b. Customer (noninterbank) foreign currency loans	21	16	76	12	57
5. *Sensitivity to market risks*					
5.1 Ratio of gross foreign currency assets to own funds	21	6	29	2	10
a. Gross foreign currency assets	21	16	76	10	48
5.2 Ratio of net foreign currency position to own funds	21	7	33	3	14
a. Gross foreign currency assets	21	16	76	10	48
b. Gross foreign currency liabilities	21	16	76	9	43
c. Net off-balance-sheet foreign currency positions (nominal value) not included above	21	10	48	2	10
5.3 Average interest rate repricing period for assets	21	6	29	1	5
5.4 Average interest rate repricing period for liabilities	21	6	29	1	5
5.5 Duration of assets	21	5	24	1	5
5.6 Duration of liabilities	21	5	24	0	0
5.7 Ratio of gross positions in equities to own funds	21	8	38	2	10
a. Gross holdings of equities	21	17	81	11	52
5.8 Ratio of net positions in equities to own funds	21	6	29	3	14
a. Gross holdings of equities	21	17	81	11	52
b. Net off-balance-sheet nominal-value position in equities, not included above	21	8	38	2	10
5.9 Ratio of gross position in commodities to own funds	21	3	14	1	5
a. Gross asset position in commodities	21	6	29	1	5
5.10 Ratio of net position in commodities to own funds	21	5	24	2	10
a. Gross asset position in commodities	21	6	29	1	5
b. Net off-balance-sheet nominal-value position in commodities, not included above	21	7	33	2	10

Emerging Countries					Developing Countries					World Total				
Total in Group	Number Compiling FSIs	Percent of Total	Number Disseminating FSIs	Percent of Total	Total in Group	Number Compiling FSIs	Percent of Total	Number Disseminating FSIs	Percent of Total	Total in Group	Number Compiling FSIs	Percent of Total	Number Disseminating FSIs	Percent of Total
44	10	23	4	9	28	5	18	1	4	93	18	19	5	5
44	25	57	11	25	28	13	46	8	29	93	46	49	20	22
44	21	48	8	18	28	10	36	7	25	93	37	40	16	17
44	19	43	9	20	28	9	32	7	25	93	32	34	17	18
44	16	36	7	16	28	9	32	7	25	93	29	31	14	15
44	10	23	4	9	28	5	18	1	4	93	18	19	5	5
44	26	59	11	25	28	13	46	8	29	93	47	51	20	22
44	21	48	7	16	28	10	36	7	25	93	37	40	15	16
44	21	48	9	20	28	9	32	7	25	93	34	37	17	18
44	16	36	6	14	28	9	32	7	25	93	29	31	13	14
44	20	45	15	34	28	6	21	5	18	93	33	35	24	26
44	15	34	8	18	28	7	25	6	21	93	25	27	14	15
44	8	18	4	9	28	6	21	3	11	93	20	22	11	12
44	34	77	24	55	28	15	54	11	39	93	67	72	49	53
44	33	75	25	57	28	18	64	14	50	93	69	74	53	57
44	15	34	8	18	28	7	25	2	7	93	33	35	14	15
44	37	84	32	73	28	23	82	13	46	93	79	85	60	65
44	39	89	32	73	28	25	89	14	50	93	83	89	61	66
44	13	30	6	14	28	4	14	1	4	93	24	26	11	12
44	35	80	23	52	28	18	64	10	36	93	69	74	45	48
44	35	80	22	50	28	19	68	10	36	93	70	75	44	47
44	14	32	6	14	28	4	14	1	4	93	24	26	9	10
44	37	84	20	45	28	19	68	11	39	93	72	77	41	44
44	14	32	7	16	28	4	14	1	4	93	25	27	11	12
44	36	82	21	48	28	19	68	10	36	93	71	76	41	44
44	36	82	21	48	28	20	71	10	36	93	72	77	40	43
44	25	57	12	27	28	15	54	8	29	93	50	54	22	24
44	9	20	2	5	28	2	7	1	4	93	17	18	4	4
44	9	20	2	5	28	1	4	0	0	93	16	17	3	3
44	11	25	6	14	28	6	21	2	7	93	22	24	9	10
44	10	23	5	11	28	6	21	2	7	93	21	23	7	8
44	8	18	5	11	28	5	18	1	4	93	21	23	8	9
44	25	57	14	32	28	13	46	7	25	93	55	59	32	34
44	7	16	4	9	28	2	7	1	4	93	15	16	8	9
44	22	50	13	30	28	12	43	6	21	93	51	55	30	32
44	11	25	7	16	28	6	218	4	14	93	25	27	13	14
44	3	7	1	2	28	1	4	0	0	93	7	8	2	2
44	7	16	5	11	28	2	7	0	0	93	15	16	6	6
44	2	5	1	2	28	1	4	0	0	93	8	9	3	3
44	6	14	4	9	28	2	7	0	0	93	14	15	5	5
44	6	14	4	9	28	2	7	0	0	93	15	16	6	6

Appendix V   Survey on the Use, Compilation, and Dissemination of Macroprudential Indicators

At the request of its Executive Board, the IMF is conducting a survey of needs and practices related to macroprudential indicators (MPIs)—defined broadly as indicators of the health and stability of financial institutions and of their corporate and household counterparties. The purpose of the survey is to gather information on the use of macroprudential data and on country practices in compiling and disseminating the data. Survey results will be used to identify a set of statistical measures that can be regularly monitored by national authorities in their financial sector assessment work, by the IMF in its surveillance activities, and ultimately by the private sector.

The survey covers the use, compilation, and dissemination of aggregate data on the financial system, and does not cover information on individual institutions. The survey is intended to solicit the views of respondents and is *not* intended to gather the actual numerical data on MPIs. All responses are confidential. No information will be released in a form that allows public identification of individual country responses.

Work by the IMF on MPIs is part of ongoing efforts in the international community to strengthen the architecture of the global financial system. Among the institutions to initiate action in this area, the IMF has been called upon to assess financial system soundness as part of its surveillance work—a process now under way as part of the joint World Bank-IMF Financial Sector Assessment Program (FSAP), introduced in May 1999. The ability to monitor financial soundness presupposes the availability of valid indicators of the health and stability of financial systems—or MPIs. MPIs allow for assessments based on objective measures of financial soundness. If comparable across countries—through adherence to internationally agreed prudential, accounting, and statistical standards—they facilitate monitoring at the global level and permit comparisons of national conditions with global benchmarks. If made publicly available, they enhance access to key financial information and can contribute to strengthening of market discipline.

The focus of this survey is on indicators of the current health of the financial system, which are primarily derived by aggregating data on the soundness of individual financial institutions. For practical purposes, the survey limits itself to the depository corporations (banking) sector and to their corporate and household counterparties. This focus is appropriate for a first-time survey in this area, but it is recognized that further research is needed on the effects of nondepository financial institutions and securities markets on financial stability.

MPIs are only one of the tools of macroprudential analysis. The assessment of financial system soundness involves coupling the analysis of MPIs with macroeconomic data on overall economic conditions, information on other financial institutions and markets, and qualitative information about the institutional, policy, and regulatory environment. A variety of techniques can be used in macroprudential analysis, including stress tests, sensitivity analysis, and other methodologies.

Instructions for Completing the Survey

The survey is being sent to the central banks of all IMF member countries. The survey has two major parts, which are addressed to different organizations in your country. We would like to request the assistance of your institution in identifying the appropriate respondents for each part of the survey, forwarding the questionnaires, and collecting the responses (see below). We would appreciate the return of the completed survey to us by July 28, 2000.

Part I: User Questionnaire. This questionnaire is addressed to (1) financial sector supervisors, (2) analysts and policy officials within the central bank or other government authorities involved in the analysis of financial system soundness, and (3) financial market participants and analysts in academia or the private sector. Six copies of the user questionnaire are provided, for distribution by the central bank. The central bank may find it useful to select respondents based on their ability to contribute to a balanced depiction of the needs for MPIs in the country. In order to protect the confidentiality of private sector and academic respondents, we would like to request that the central bank prepare an overview of their responses, which should be returned to the IMF.

Part I (a): User Questionnaire: Covers usefulness of specific MPIs and requirements for frequency of compilation.

Part I (b): Supplementary Issues: Covers additional questions related to the needs for, and analysis of, MPIs.

Part II: Compilation and Dissemination Questionnaire. This questionnaire is intended for staff within the monetary or supervisory authorities, or other government institutions, responsible for the compilation of MPIs and components of MPIs, and for their dissemination to the public, where appropriate. The selection of the respondents will depend upon the institutional setup in each country.

Part II (a): Compilation and Dissemination Questionnaire: Covers practices related to the compilation and dissemination of MPIs or components of MPIs.

Part II (b): Supplementary Issues: Covers technical questions on factors affecting the compilation and dissemination of MPIs or components of MPIs.

Part II (c): Valuation Issues: Covers valuation practices affecting MPIs or components of MPIs.

Coverage: The survey covers the depository corporations subsector, which corresponds roughly to the banking sector. It includes all major divisions of depository corporations, including commercial banks, branches and subsidiaries of foreign banks operating in your country, money market funds that issue deposit-like shares, foreign currency and foreign trade banks, international banking facilities, investment banks, mortgage banking institutions, credit unions, specialized banks, and others as appropriate. Government-owned or -controlled depository corporations are included. For the purpose of this survey, the central bank is excluded. Mutual funds whose liabilities to investors are close substitutes for bank deposits should be included in the survey, but other mutual funds should be excluded.

MPIs and MPI components: The questionnaires list a number of aggregate indicators that, based on surveillance and empirical work at the IMF and else-

where, are considered useful for assessing the health and stability of financial systems. The survey also gathers information on components of MPIs to ascertain whether the underlying information exists to compile MPIs that are not now being compiled. The exact definitions of each indicator or its components may vary from country to country. Respondents are kindly asked to indicate cases where the MPIs used or available are similar to, but not identical to, those presented in the survey.

Special issues pages: The User Questionnaire and the Compilation and Dissemination Questionnaire each include a page devoted to a series of questions on special issues related to MPIs.

Additional comments: Respondents may wish to provide supplemental information important for the analysis of financial stability conditions in their country, important indicators not listed in the survey, special conditions that affect compilation and dissemination of MPIs, and alternatives to the definitions and descriptions of MPIs provided in the survey. "Comments" cells for this purpose corresponding to each MPI have been created on the User Questionnaire, Part I (a), and spaces for general comments are provided at the ends of the User Questionnaire Part I (a) and the Compilation and Dissemination Questionnaire Part II (a). Other comments may be entered elsewhere in the spreadsheets by right-clicking your mouse button to select "Insert Comment."

Optional reports on other financial institutions and markets: Central banks may also choose to provide separate reports for other financial institutions or markets that are important for the analysis of overall financial stability conditions in their countries. When doing so, please describe the types of institutions or markets covered and why they are important for macroprudential analysis.

Returning the questionnaire: Responses should be sent to the IMF by July 28, 2000:

— by Internet to: f2survey@imf.org

— or by mail (diskette or paper copy) to:

MPI Survey
Financial Institutions Division II
Statistics Department
International Monetary Fund
700 19th Street, N.W.
Washington, D.C. 20431, USA

Contacts regarding the survey: IMF staff may contact you regarding the survey to better understand your needs and compilation practices related to MPIs, or to clarify your responses.

MPI Survey: Explanation of Terms

Disclaimer: This glossary is provided for the convenience of the recipients of this survey. The explanations of the terms may not correspond to official definitions or standards.

Bid-Ask Spread. Difference between the prices at which a market participant is willing to buy and sell a security, such as a Treasury security.

Basel Capital. Capital as defined in the 1988 Capital Accord of the Basel Committee on Banking Supervision and subsequent revisions. The Accord defines three capital elements. Tier 1 capital consists of permanent shareholders' equity and disclosed reserves; tier 2 capital consists of undisclosed reserves, revaluation reserves, general provisions and loan-loss reserves, hybrid debt-equity capital instruments, and subordinated long-term debt (over five years); tier 3 capital consists of subordinated short-term debt (over two years).

Basel Capital Adequacy Ratio. The ratio of capital, as defined above, divided by risk-weighted assets. Risk-weighted assets equals the sum of each category of asset (and on-balance-sheet equivalents for off-balance-sheet positions) multiplied by a weight representing the credit risk associated with each category.

Basel Capital Deductions. Under the Basel Capital Accord, supervisors may require depository corporations to deduct certain items—such as investments in non-consolidated financial subsidiaries—from capital in order to calculate capital adequacy ratios.

Capital. Sum of equity capital and reserves. It is the amount by which assets exceed liabilities.

Consolidation. Refers to the elimination of stocks and flows between institutional units when they are grouped. In particular, a headquarters office and its branch offices and subsidiaries would report stock and flow data consolidated in a single statement. Global consolidation refers to the elimination of stocks and flows occurring across all offices regardless of their country of location. National consolidation refers to the elimination of stocks and flows occurring across all offices that are residents of a specific country.

Credit. Comprises assets for which the counterparty incurs debt liabilities. Includes loans, securities other than shares, and miscellaneous receivables. Equity instruments, financial derivatives, and lines of credit are excluded.

Debt Service. Repayments of principal and interest on mortgages or other outstanding debt.

Depository Corporation. Financial institutions that engage in banking-type activities, whether or not they are called banks or are subject to supervision by a regulatory/supervisory office. The standard statistical definition includes the central bank and other depository corporations, described below, but for the purposes of this survey, the central bank is excluded.

Duration. Weighted average term-to-maturity of an asset's cash flow, the weights being the present value of each future cash flow as a percentage of the asset's full price.

Equity Capital. Issued and fully paid ordinary shares/common stock and noncumulative perpetual preferred stock (but excluding cumulative preferred stock).

Financial Derivative (or derivative instrument). Contract whose value is based on the performance of an underlying financial asset, index, or other investment.

Global Consolidation. An accounting statement including all parts of an enterprise regardless of their locations worldwide (see Consolidation).

Gross Asset (or Liability) Position in Derivatives. The on-balance-sheet value of derivatives in an asset (or liability) position, plus the fair value of off-balance-sheet derivatives in an asset (or liability) position.

Interest Income, Net. Difference between the interest income produced by a financial institution's earning assets (loans and investments) and its interest expenses.

Loans. Financial assets (1) that are created when a creditor lends funds directly to a debtor; (2) that are evidenced by nonnegotiable documents; or (3) for which no security is issued as evidence of the transaction.

Mortgage. Loans under which the borrower gives the lender a lien on the property (usually real estate) as collateral for repayment of the loan.

National Consolidation. An accounting statement encompassing all parts of an enterprise within a country, but excluding branches and subsidiaries outside the country (see Consolidation).

Net Position. Refers to gross holdings, less gross liabilities, plus net positions under derivatives or other financial commitments in currencies, other financial instruments, or commodities. For example, a net foreign currency position equals gross foreign currency-denominated assets, less gross foreign currency-denominated liabilities, plus the net position under foreign currency financial derivatives and other financial commitments.

Nominal Value of Financial Derivatives. The stated contract value of the underlying item delivered under a financial derivative. For example, an option that has a nominal value of 100,000 francs will deliver 100,000 francs when exercised.

Nonperforming Loan (NPL). A loan is said to be nonperforming when the principal and/or interest payments on it according to the original terms of the borrower's loan agreement are past due (e.g., by 90 days or more).

Operating Costs. The sum of interest and noninterest (fees and commissions, trading losses, and salary and other current costs) expenses.

Other Depository Corporations. Banks (other than the central bank) and similar institutions that carry out banking functions with the public. A full definition is provided in the System of National Accounts 1993. The definition corresponds with monetary financial institutions as defined in the European System of Account 1995. It includes a variety of institutions regardless of whether they are called banks or are subject to banking supervision, including commercial banks, branches, and subsidiaries of foreign banks operating in the country, money market funds that issue deposit-like shares, foreign currency and foreign trade banks, international banking facilities, investment banks, Islamic banks, mortgage banking institutions, credit unions, spe-cialized banks, and others as appropriate. Government-owned or -controlled depository corporations are included. Mutual funds whose liabilities to investors are close substitutes for bank deposits are included, but other mutual funds are excluded.

Own Funds. Equity capital and reserves.

Profits. Sum remaining after all expenses have been met or deducted from income. Both pretax and post-tax concepts are used.

Reference Rate. A specific lending or borrowing rate considered representative of overall rates that is used as a benchmark for evaluating conditions in interest rate markets.

Related Entities. Affiliated enterprises, owners and management of an enterprise, and individuals related to owners and managers.

Repricing Period for Interest Rates. The average period (usually expressed in months) until existing financial instruments are redeemed or until the interest rates on financial instruments are reset or reindexed.

Turnover. Volume of securities traded during a period (e.g., daily) as a percentage of total securities listed on an exchange.

Table A5.1. MPI Survey — Part I (a): User Questionnaire

Check type of user: Supervisor _____
Policy/Research _____
Market Participant/Other _____

MPI	Is aggregate information on this MPI useful? 4 – very useful 3 – useful 2 – sometimes useful 1 – not useful X – no opinion	How frequently should this MPI be compiled to meet users' needs? M – monthly Q – quarterly S – semi-annually A – annually O – other (specify)	Comments
1. *Capital adequacy*			
1.1 Basel capital adequacy ratio			
1.1a Ratio of Basel tier I capital to risk-weighted assets			
1.1b Ratio of Basel tier I + tier II capital to risk-weighted assets			
1.1c Ratio of Basel tier I + II + III capital to risk-weighted assets			
1.2 Distribution of capital adequacy ratios (number of institutions within specified capital adequacy ratio ranges)			
1.3 Ratio of total on-balance-sheet assets to own funds			
2. *Asset quality*			
(a) Lending institution			
2.1 Distribution of on-balance-sheet assets, by Basel risk-weight category			
2.2 Ratio of total gross asset position in financial derivatives to own funds			
2.3 Ratio of total gross liability position in financial derivatives to own funds			
2.4 Distribution of loans by sector			
2.4a *of which:* for investment in commercial real estate			
2.4b *of which:* for investment in residential real estate			
2.5 Distribution of credit extended by sector			
2.6 Distribution of credit extended by country or region			
2.7 Ratio of credit to related entities to total credit			
2.8 Ratio of total large loans to own funds			
2.9 Ratio of gross nonperforming loans to total assets			
2.10 Ratio of nonperforming loans net of provisions to total assets			
(b) Borrowing institution			
2.11 Ratio of corporate debt to own funds ("debt-equity ratio")			
2.12 Ratio of corporate profits to equity			
2.13 Ratio of corporate debt service costs to total corporate income			
2.14 Corporate net foreign currency exposure			
2.15 Ratio of household total debt to GDP			
2.15a *of which:* mortgage debt to GDP			
2.15b *of which:* debt owed to depository corporations to GDP			
2.16 Number of applications for protection from creditors			
3. *Profitability and competitiveness*			
3.1 Rate of change in number of depository corporations			
3.2 Ratio of profits to period-average assets (ROA)			
3.3 Ratio of profits to period-average equity (ROE)			
3.4 Ratio of net interest income to total income			
3.5 Ratio of trading and foreign exchange gains/losses to total income			

3.6 Ratio of operating costs to net interest income
3.7 Ratio of staff costs to operating costs
3.8 Spread between reference lending and deposit rates
3.9 Share of assets of the three largest depository corporations in total assets of depository corporations

4. Liquidity

4.1 Distribution of three-month local-currency interbank rates for different depository corporations
4.2 Average interbank bid-ask spread for three-month local-currency deposits
4.3 Ratio of liquid assets to total assets
4.4 Ratio of liquid assets to liquid liabilities
4.5 Average maturity of assets
4.6 Average maturity of liabilities
4.7 Average daily turnover in the treasury bill (or central bank bill) market
4.8 Average bid-ask spread in the treasury bill (or central bank bill) market
4.9 Ratio of central bank credit to depository corporations to depository corporations' total liabilities
4.10 Ratio of customer deposits to total (noninterbank) loans
4.11 Ratio of customer foreign currency deposits to total (noninterbank) foreign currency loans

5. Sensitivity to market risks

5.1 Ratio of gross foreign currency assets to own funds
5.2 Ratio of net foreign currency position to own funds
5.3 Average interest rate repricing period for assets
5.4 Average interest rate repricing period for liabilities
5.5 Duration of assets
5.6 Duration of liabilities
5.7 Ratio of gross equity position to own funds
5.8 Ratio of net equity position to own funds
5.9 Ratio of gross position in commodities to own funds
5.10 Ratio of net position in commodities to own funds

Additional Comments: This space is for any additional comments you may wish to provide, such as MPIs or topics you address that are not covered in the survey, MPIs defined differently than in the survey, or concerns over data quality or availability. We are also interested in views regarding MPIs or topics that are not relevant for your needs or that are seen as impractical.

Table A5.2. MPI Survey—Part I (b): Supplementary Issues

1. Macroprudential research

Are you carrying out, or planning, research on the health and stability of the financial system? Is this research focused on the condition of individual institutions, the banking sector as a whole, or other sectors? What analytical or statistical frameworks are employed in this research?

2. Coverage of financial institutions

a. Other important institutions, markets, and financial activities

In addition to depository corporations, what other markets, institutions, and financial activities are important in the overall analysis of the soundness and condition of the financial sector?

b. Aggregation of depository institutions

Within the definition of "depository corporations" used in this survey, is there a need for further disaggregation or special analysis of specific subsectors—for example, for foreign banks, international banking facilities, internationally active banks as covered under the Basel standards, mutual funds, or others?

c. Systemically important institutions

What techniques are used to evaluate the condition of systemically important institutions in your country? How are systemically important institutions identified? Are they subject to enhanced statistical requirements or disclosure requirements?

3. MPI norms, benchmarks, and thresholds
What norms or benchmark levels or ranges are used for MPIs? Have values been identified for warning level thresholds?

4. Presentation of MPIs
Please indicate your preferences regarding the mode for presentation of MPIs (e.g., as single point estimates, ratios, growth rates, measures of dispersion, standard deviations, etc.).

5. Composite measures
Please indicate whether you use, or plan to use, composite measures of the condition of the financial system. What types of information are used to construct such measures?

6. Business surveys
Do you make use of business survey results (general surveys of business sentiment or specialized surveys on financial institutions) to supplement your analysis of MPIs?

Table A5.3. MPI Survey—Part II (a): Compilation and Dissemination Questionnaire

	Compilation	
	Periodicity M – monthly Q – quarterly S – semi- annually A – annually O – other (specify) X – not compiled	Timeliness Average number of working days after reference period X - not compiled
MPIs and Components		

1. *Capital adequacy*

1.1 Basel capital adequacy ratio
   a. Basel tier I capital (net of deductions)
   b. Basel tier II capital (net of deductions)
   c. Basel tier III capital (net of deductions)
   d. Risk-weighted assets

1.2 Distribution of capital adequacy ratios
   a. Number of institutions with Basel capital ratios falling into
      specified ranges:
      Specify range used: ____ % *to* ____ %, *etc.*   *specify*
   b. Assets of institutions within each range
   c. Assets by type of depository corporation:
      c.1 Headquartered in the country
        of which: internationally active
        of which: state-owned or -controlled
      c.2 Headquartered in other countries

1.3 Ratio of total on-balance-sheet assets to own funds
   a. Total on-balance-sheet assets
   b. Own funds (equity capital and reserves)

2. *Asset quality*

(a) Lending institution

2.1 Distribution of on-balance-sheet assets by Basel risk-weight category
   a. Assets per Basel risk-weight category

2.2 Ratio of total gross asset position in financial derivatives to own funds
   a. Total gross asset position in derivatives
   b. *of which:* off-balance-sheet position

2.3 Ratio of total gross liability position in financial derivatives to own funds
   a. Total gross liability position in derivatives
   b. *of which:* off-balance-sheet position

2.4 Distribution of loans by sector
   a. Loans by national account sectors
      of which:
      a.1. Loans for investment in commercial real estate
      a.2. Loans for investment in residential real estate
      a.3. Loans to other key sectors   *specify*
   b. Total loans

2.5 Distribution of credit extended by sector
   a. Credit by national account sectors
   b. Total credit

2.6 Distribution of credit by country or region
   a. Loans by country or region

2.7 Ratio of credit to related entities to total credit
   a. Credit to related entities

2.8 Ratio of total large loans to own funds
   a. Total large loans (specify size range)   *specify*

2.9 Ratio of gross nonperforming loans to total assets
   a. Gross nonperforming loans

2.10 Ratio of nonperforming loans net of provisions to total assets
   a. Nonperforming loans net of provisions

Dissemination		Data Sources		
Periodicity	Timeliness	Supervisory	Statistical	Other (specify)
M – monthly				
Q – quarterly			(Indicate type of consolidation used)	
S – semi- annually			G = global consolidation	
A – annually	Average number of working		N = national consolidation	
O – other (specify)	days after reference period		B = both national and global consolidation	
X – not disseminated	X - not disseminated			

Table A5.3 (continued)

	Compilation	
	Periodicity M – monthly Q – quarterly S – semi- annually A – annually O – other (specify) X – not compiled	**Timeliness** Average number of working days after reference period X - not compiled
MPIs and Components		

(b)   Borrowing institution

2.11 Ratio of corporate debt to own funds ("debt-equity ratio")
  a. Total corporate debt
  b. Corporations' own funds

2.12 Ratio of corporate profits to equity
  a. Corporate pre-tax profits
  b. Corporate post-tax profits

2.13 Ratio of corporate debt service costs to profits
  a. Corporate debt service costs

2.14 Corporate net foreign currency exposure
  a. Gross foreign currency assets
  b. Gross foreign currency liabilities
  c. Net off-balance-sheet foreign currency positions (nominal value)
      not included above

2.15 Ratio of household debt to GDP
  a. Household total debt
  b. *of which:* mortgage debt
  c. *of which:* debt to depository corporations

2.16 Number of applications for protection from creditors

3.   *Profitability and competitiveness*

3.1 Rate of change in the number of depository corporations
  a. Difference between number of institutions at beginning and end of period
  b. *of which:* due to mergers and acquisitions
  c. *of which:* due to withdrawals of licenses or closing of units

3.2 Ratios of profits to period-average assets (ROA)
  a. Pretax, after provisions profits
  b. Posttax profits
  c. Total period-average on-balance-sheet assets

3.3 Ratios of profits to period-average equity (ROE)
  a. Pretax, after provisions profits
  b. Posttax profits
  c. Period-average equity

3.4 Ratio of net interest income to profits
  a. Net interest income

3.5 Ratio of trading and foreign-currency gains/losses to profits
  a. Gains/losses in securities and foreign currencies

3.6 Ratio of operating costs to net interest income
  a. Operating costs

3.7 Ratio of staff costs to operating costs
  a. Staff costs

3.8 Spreads between reference lending and deposit rates
  a. Reference lending rate   *specify*
  b. Reference deposit rate   *specify*

3.9 Share of assets of the three largest depository corporations in total
     assets of depository corporations
  a. Assets of the three largest depository corporations

Dissemination		Data Sources		
Periodicity	Timeliness	Supervisory	Statistical	Other (specify)
M – monthly				
Q – quarterly			(Indicate type of consolidation used)	
S – semi- annually		G = global consolidation		
A – annually	Average number of working	N = national consolidation		
O – other (specify)	days after reference period	B = both national and global consolidation		
X – not disseminated	X - not disseminated			

Table A5.3 *(continued)*

	Compilation	
MPIs and Components	Periodicity M – monthly Q – quarterly S – semi- annually A – annually O – other (specify) X – not compiled	Timeliness Average number of working days after reference period X - not compiled
4. *Liquidity*		
4.1 Distribution of three-month local-currency interbank rates for different banks	_____	_____
4.2 Average interbank bid-ask spread for three-month local currency interbank deposits	_____	_____
4.3 Ratio of liquid assets to total assets 　a. Liquid assets	_____ _____	_____ _____
4.4 Ratio of liquid assets to liquid liabilities 　a. Liquid liabilities	_____ _____	_____ _____
4.5 Average maturity of assets 　a. Average remaining maturity of assets (months) 　b. *of which:* foreign currency assets 　c. Average original maturity of assets (months) 　d. *of which:* foreign currency assets	_____ _____ _____ _____	_____ _____ _____ _____
4.6 Average maturity of liabilities 　a. Average remaining maturity of liabilities (months) 　b. *of which:* foreign currency liabilities 　c. Average original maturity of liabilities (months) 　d. *of which:* foreign currency liabilities	_____ _____ _____ _____	_____ _____ _____ _____
4.7 Average daily turnover in the Treasury bill (or central bank bill) market	_____	_____
4.8 Average bid-ask spread in the Treasury bil (or central bank bill) market	_____	_____
4.9 Ratio of central bank credit to depository corporations to their total liabilities 　a. Total credit from the central bank to depository corporations 　b. Total liabilities	_____ _____ _____	_____ _____ _____
4.10 Ratio of total customer deposits to total (noninterbank) loans 　a. Customer (noninterbank) deposits 　b. Total (noninterbank) loans	_____ _____ _____	_____ _____ _____
4.11 Ratio of foreign currency customer deposits to total (noninterbank) foreign currency loans 　a. Customer (noninterbank) foreign currency deposits 　b. Customer (noninterbank) foreign currency loans	_____ _____ _____	_____ _____ _____
5. *Sensitivity to market risks*		
5.1 Ratio of gross foreign currency assets to own funds 　a. Gross foreign currency assets	_____ _____	_____ _____
5.2 Ratio of net foreign currency position to own funds 　a. Gross foreign currency assets 　b. Gross foreign currency liabilities 　c. Net off-balance-sheet foreign currency positions (nominal value) not included above	_____ _____ _____ _____	_____ _____ _____ _____
5.3 Average interest rate repricing period for assets	_____	_____
5.4 Average interest rate repricing period for liabilities	_____	_____
5.5 Duration of assets	_____	_____
5.6 Duration of liabilities	_____	_____
5.7 Ratio of gross position in equities to own funds 　a. Gross holdings of equities	_____ _____	_____ _____

| Dissemination | | Data Sources | | |
Periodicity	Timeliness	Supervisory	Statistical	Other (specify)
M – monthly				
Q – quarterly			(Indicate type of consolidation used)	
S – semi- annually			G = global consolidation	
A – annually	Average number of working		N = national consolidation	
O – other (specify)	days after reference period		B = both national and global consolidation	
X – not disseminated	X - not disseminated			

Table A5.3 (concluded)

	Compilation	
	Periodicity M – monthly Q – quarterly S – semi- annually A – annually O – other (specify)	Timeliness Average number of working days after reference period
MPIs and Components	X – not compiled	X - not compiled
5.8 Ratio of net position in equities to own funds	_____	_____
a. Gross holdings of equities	_____	_____
b. Net off-balance-sheet nominal-value position in equities not included above	_____	_____
5.9 Ratio of gross position in commodities to own funds	_____	_____
a. Gross asset position in commodities	_____	_____
5.10 Ratio of net position in commodities to own funds	_____	_____
a. Gross asset position in commodities	_____	_____
b. Net off-balance-sheet nominal-value position in commodities, not included above	_____	_____

Additional Comments: This space is for any additional comments you may wish to provide, such as MPIs or topics you address that are not covered in the survey, MPIs defined differently than in the survey, or concerns over data quality or availability. We are also interested in views regarding MPIs or topics that are not relevant for your needs or that are seen as impractical.

Dissemination		Data Sources		
Periodicity	Timeliness	Supervisory	Statistical	Other (specify)
M – monthly				
Q – quarterly				
S – semi- annually		(Indicate type of consolidation used)		
A – annually	Average number of working	G = global consolidation		
O – other (specify)	days after reference period	N = national consolidation		
X – not disseminated	X - not disseminated	B = both national and global consolidation		

Table A5.4. MPI Survey—Part II (b): Supplementary Issues

1. Institutional coverage
a. Supervisory responsibility over financial institutions
Please list the institutions that have supervisory responsibility for various segments of the financial system and financial activities.

b. Institutional coverage
Please specify the institutional coverage *for each data source* (e.g., supervisory, statistical, other). Coverage of branches and subsidiaries of foreign financial institutions operating in the country should be described. Also describe coverage of offshore banking operations.

2. Loan classification and provisioning rules
a. Classification rules
Please describe the system for grading nonperforming loans.

b. Income recognition/interest accrual rules
Please describe practices and standards for recognition of income, accrual of interest, or other changes in value.

c. Loan-loss provisioning rules
Please describe the rules governing the recognition and valuation of provisions.

d. Collateral
Please describe requirements and valuation rules for collateral (including real estate).

3. Capital classification rules
Please describe the components of tier I, tier II, and (if applicable) tier III capital, and the deductions for each category.

4. Other issues
Please describe practices for recognition and instrument classification for repurchase agreements, securities lending, bankers' acceptances, and financial derivatives.

5. Real estate lending
Please describe the categories of lending that are recorded as real estate lending, such as loans for the purpose of real estate construction, loans to construction companies, loans collateralized by real estate, mortgage loans, etc. What real estate price information is available?

6. Data dissemination
a. Restrictions on dissemination of aggregated data
Please describe legal and other restrictions on the dissemination of the MPIs and their components to the public.

b. Restrictions on dissemination of individual institutions' data
Please describe legal and other restrictions on the disclosure of information on individual financial institutions (including any restrictions on provision of information to the IMF).

Table A5.5. MPI Survey—Part II (c): Valuation Issues

	Price		Foreign Currency-Denominated Instruments	
	Reference price H = historic cost M = market price/fair value L = lower of cost or market O = other (specify)	Frequency of revaluations B = on-balance-sheet date O = other (specify)	Conversion exchange rate E = market rate (end period) A = market rate (per. average) G = official rate O = other (specify)	Frequency of revaluations B = on-balance-sheet date O = other (specify)
1. Supervisory Data Sources				
a. Deposits				
b. Loans				
c. Securities (other than shares)				
d. Shares and other equity				
e. Financial derivatives				
f. Miscellaneous receivables/payables				
g. Nonfinancial assets (real estate and other assets)				
2. Statistical Data Sources				
a. Deposits				
b. Loans				
c. Securities (other than shares)				
d. Shares and other equity				
e. Financial derivatives				
f. Miscellaneous receivables/payables				
g. Nonfinancial assets (real estate and other assets)				
3. Other Data Sources				
a. Deposits				
b. Loans				
c. Securities (other than shares)				
d. Shares and other equity				
e. Financial derivatives				
f. Miscellaneous receivables/payables				
g. Nonfinancial assets (real estate and other assets)				

Recent Occasional Papers of the International Monetary Fund

212. Financial Soundness Indicators: Analytical Aspects and Country Practices, by V. Sundararajan, Charles Enoch, Armida San José, Paul Hilbers, Russell Krueger, Marina Moretti, and Graham Slack. 2002.

211. Capital Account Liberalization and Financial Sector Stability, by a staff team led by Shogo Ishii and Karl Habermeier. 2002.

210. IMF-Supported Programs in Capital Account Crises, by Atish Ghosh, Timothy Lane, Marianne Schulze-Ghattas, Aleš Bulíř, Javier Hamann, and Alex Mourmouras. 2002.

209. Methodology for Current Account and Exchange Rate Assessments, by Peter Isard, Hamid Faruqee, G. Russell Kincaid, and Martin Fetherston. 2001.

208. Yemen in the 1990s: From Unification to Economic Reform, by Klaus Enders, Sherwyn Williams, Nada Choueiri, Yuri Sobolev, and Jan Walliser. 2001.

207. Malaysia: From Crisis to Recovery, by Kanitta Meesook, Il Houng Lee, Olin Liu, Yougesh Khatri, Natalia Tamirisa, Michael Moore, and Mark H. Krysl. 2001.

206. The Dominican Republic: Stabilization, Structural Reform, and Economic Growth, by Alessandro Giustiniani, Werner C. Keller, and Randa E. Sab. 2001.

205. Stabilization and Savings Funds for Nonrenewable Resources, by Jeffrey Davis, Rolando Ossowski, James Daniel, and Steven Barnett. 2001.

204. Monetary Union in West Africa (ECOWAS): Is It Desirable and How Could It Be Achieved? by Paul Masson and Catherine Pattillo. 2001.

203. Modern Banking and OTC Derivatives Markets: The Transformation of Global Finance and Its Implications for Systemic Risk, by Garry J. Schinasi, R. Sean Craig, Burkhard Drees, and Charles Kramer. 2000.

202. Adopting Inflation Targeting: Practical Issues for Emerging Market Countries, by Andrea Schaechter, Mark R. Stone, and Mark Zelmer. 2000.

201. Developments and Challenges in the Caribbean Region, by Samuel Itam, Simon Cueva, Erik Lundback, Janet Stotsky, and Stephen Tokarick. 2000.

200. Pension Reform in the Baltics: Issues and Prospects, by Jerald Schiff, Niko Hobdari, Axel Schimmelpfennig, and Roman Zytek. 2000.

199. Ghana: Economic Development in a Democratic Environment, by Sérgio Pereira Leite, Anthony Pellechio, Luisa Zanforlin, Girma Begashaw, Stefania Fabrizio, and Joachim Harnack. 2000.

198. Setting Up Treasuries in the Baltics, Russia, and Other Countries of the Former Soviet Union: An Assessment of IMF Technical Assistance, by Barry H. Potter and Jack Diamond. 2000.

197. Deposit Insurance: Actual and Good Practices, by Gillian G.H. Garcia. 2000.

196. Trade and Trade Policies in Eastern and Southern Africa, by a staff team led by Arvind Subramanian, with Enrique Gelbard, Richard Harmsen, Katrin Elborgh-Woytek, and Piroska Nagy. 2000.

195. The Eastern Caribbean Currency Union—Institutions, Performance, and Policy Issues, by Frits van Beek, José Roberto Rosales, Mayra Zermeño, Ruby Randall, and Jorge Shepherd. 2000.

194. Fiscal and Macroeconomic Impact of Privatization, by Jeffrey Davis, Rolando Ossowski, Thomas Richardson, and Steven Barnett. 2000.

193. Exchange Rate Regimes in an Increasingly Integrated World Economy, by Michael Mussa, Paul Masson, Alexander Swoboda, Esteban Jadresic, Paolo Mauro, and Andy Berg. 2000.

192. Macroprudential Indicators of Financial System Soundness, by a staff team led by Owen Evans, Alfredo M. Leone, Mahinder Gill, and Paul Hilbers. 2000.

191. Social Issues in IMF-Supported Programs, by Sanjeev Gupta, Louis Dicks-Mireaux, Ritha Khemani, Calvin McDonald, and Marijn Verhoeven. 2000.

190. Capital Controls: Country Experiences with Their Use and Liberalization, by Akira Ariyoshi, Karl Habermeier, Bernard Laurens, Inci Ötker-Robe, Jorge Iván Canales Kriljenko, and Andrei Kirilenko. 2000.

189. Current Account and External Sustainability in the Baltics, Russia, and Other Countries of the Former Soviet Union, by Donal McGettigan. 2000.

188. Financial Sector Crisis and Restructuring: Lessons from Asia, by Carl-Johan Lindgren, Tomás J.T. Baliño, Charles Enoch, Anne-Marie Gulde, Marc Quintyn, and Leslie Teo. 1999.

187. Philippines: Toward Sustainable and Rapid Growth, Recent Developments and the Agenda Ahead, by Markus Rodlauer, Prakash Loungani, Vivek Arora, Charalambos Christofides, Enrique G. De la Piedra, Piyabha Kongsamut, Kristina Kostial, Victoria Summers, and Athanasios Vamvakidis. 2000.

186. Anticipating Balance of Payments Crises: The Role of Early Warning Systems, by Andrew Berg, Eduardo Borensztein, Gian Maria Milesi-Ferretti, and Catherine Pattillo. 1999.

185. Oman Beyond the Oil Horizon: Policies Toward Sustainable Growth, edited by Ahsan Mansur and Volker Treichel. 1999.

184. Growth Experience in Transition Countries, 1990–98, by Oleh Havrylyshyn, Thomas Wolf, Julian Berengaut, Marta Castello-Branco, Ron van Rooden, and Valerie Mercer-Blackman. 1999.

183. Economic Reforms in Kazakhstan, Kyrgyz Republic, Tajikistan, Turkmenistan, and Uzbekistan, by Emine Gürgen, Harry Snoek, Jon Craig, Jimmy McHugh, Ivailo Izvorski, and Ron van Rooden. 1999.

182. Tax Reform in the Baltics, Russia, and Other Countries of the Former Soviet Union, by a staff team led by Liam Ebrill and Oleh Havrylyshyn. 1999.

181. The Netherlands: Transforming a Market Economy, by C. Maxwell Watson, Bas B. Bakker, Jan Kees Martijn, and Ioannis Halikias. 1999.

180. Revenue Implications of Trade Liberalization, by Liam Ebrill, Janet Stotsky, and Reint Gropp. 1999.

179. Disinflation in Transition: 1993–97, by Carlo Cottarelli and Peter Doyle. 1999.

178. IMF-Supported Programs in Indonesia, Korea, and Thailand: A Preliminary Assessment, by Timothy Lane, Atish Ghosh, Javier Hamann, Steven Phillips, Marianne Schulze-Ghattas, and Tsidi Tsikata. 1999.

177. Perspectives on Regional Unemployment in Europe, by Paolo Mauro, Eswar Prasad, and Antonio Spilimbergo. 1999.

176. Back to the Future: Postwar Reconstruction and Stabilization in Lebanon, edited by Sena Eken and Thomas Helbling. 1999.

175. Macroeconomic Developments in the Baltics, Russia, and Other Countries of the Former Soviet Union, 1992–97, by Luis M. Valdivieso. 1998.

174. Impact of EMU on Selected Non–European Union Countries, by R. Feldman, K. Nashashibi, R. Nord, P. Allum, D. Desruelle, K. Enders, R. Kahn, and H. Temprano-Arroyo. 1998.

173. The Baltic Countries: From Economic Stabilization to EU Accession, by Julian Berengaut, Augusto Lopez-Claros, Françoise Le Gall, Dennis Jones, Richard Stern, Ann-Margret Westin, Effie Psalida, Pietro Garibaldi. 1998.

172. Capital Account Liberalization: Theoretical and Practical Aspects, by a staff team led by Barry Eichengreen and Michael Mussa, with Giovanni Dell'Ariccia, Enrica Detragiache, Gian Maria Milesi-Ferretti, and Andrew Tweedie. 1998.

171. Monetary Policy in Dollarized Economies, by Tomás Baliño, Adam Bennett, and Eduardo Borensztein. 1998.

170. The West African Economic and Monetary Union: Recent Developments and Policy Issues, by a staff team led by Ernesto Hernández-Catá and comprising Christian A. François, Paul Masson, Pascal Bouvier, Patrick Peroz, Dominique Desruelle, and Athanasios Vamvakidis. 1998.

169. Financial Sector Development in Sub-Saharan African Countries, by Hassanali Mehran, Piero Ugolini, Jean Phillipe Briffaux, George Iden, Tonny Lybek, Stephen Swaray, and Peter Hayward. 1998.

168. Exit Strategies: Policy Options for Countries Seeking Greater Exchange Rate Flexibility, by a staff team led by Barry Eichengreen and Paul Masson with Hugh Bredenkamp, Barry Johnston, Javier Hamann, Esteban Jadresic, and Inci Ötker. 1998.

167. Exchange Rate Assessment: Extensions of the Macroeconomic Balance Approach, edited by Peter Isard and Hamid Faruqee. 1998.

166. Hedge Funds and Financial Market Dynamics, by a staff team led by Barry Eichengreen and Donald Mathieson with Bankim Chadha, Anne Jansen, Laura Kodres, and Sunil Sharma. 1998.

165. Algeria: Stabilization and Transition to the Market, by Karim Nashashibi, Patricia Alonso-Gamo, Stefania Bazzoni, Alain Féler, Nicole Laframboise, and Sebastian Paris Horvitz. 1998.

Note: For information on the title and availability of Occasional Papers not listed, please consult the IMF Publications Catalog or contact IMF Publication Services.